CONSUMER RIGHTS IN SERVICE SECTOR

About the Editor

V.N. Viswanathan is presently a professor of Political Science, Presidency College, Chennai. He is an eminent scholar and a well-known writer on rights based issues in India. He did his M.A. (Pol. Sc.) and M.Phil from Madurai Kamaraj University. He also did his M.A. (Pub. Admn.), B.L. and Ph.D. from University of Madras, Chennai. A prolific writer and a social activist, he provides leadership to many civil society organizations at national and regional levels in India.

CONSUMER RIGHTS IN SERVICE SECTOR

Edited by
V. N. VISWANATHAN

CONCEPT PUBLISHING COMPANY, NEW DELHI-110059

Cataloging in Publication Data—DK
Courtesy: D.K. Agencies (P) Ltd. <docinfo@dkagencies.com>

Consumer rights in service sector / edited by V.N. Viswanathan.
p. cm.
Papers presented at a national workshop held during 4-8 August 2005; in Indian context.
Includes bibliographical references.
Includes index.
ISBN 13: 9788180695315
ISBN 10: 818069531X

1. Service industries—India—Congresses. 2. Consumer protection—Law and legislation—India—Congresses. I. Viswanathan, V. N.

DDC 343.540 71 22

ISBN-13: 978-81-8069-531-5
ISBN-10: 81-8069-531-X

First Published 2008

Published and Printed by
Ashok Kumar Mittal
Concept Publishing Company
A/15-16, Commercial Block, Mohan Garden
New Delhi-110059 (INDIA)

Phones: 25351460, 25351794
Fax: 091-11-25357103
Email: publishing@conceptpub.com

Foreword

Service sector is an important area concerning society with reference to the existence, activities and welfare of its members. The various agencies which are part of this sector should perform their duties and responsibilities having regard to general and overall growth and development. When this happened the people could live a contented life. But negligence, dereliction of duty, ignorance and laxity could lead to disappointment and add to the sufferings of the people. This in turn could affect peace and tranquility in a nation. Thus, it is difficult to assess the nature of the impact and implications of performance or the non-performance or half-hearted performance of the service sector. The efforts to set right the damage caused would be an enormous task for all concerned in terms of resources needed, labour required, time that could be taken and cost of damage exercise. It is applicable to the past, present and future.

Dr. V.N. Viswanathan's effort in bringing out with himself as the chief editor of the book entitled "Consumer Rights in Service Sector" is more timely and clearly appropriate. It is generally the approach and practice for academics to trace historically the orgin, growth and utility of everything to the ancient to the present times. In this volume also some such attempt is made by one of the contributors. No doubt it is an accepted fact that the conventions, customs and some usages among the people of every society form part of as well as the basis of law or a statute that is enacted later. This also under- went modifications, alterations as circumstances warranted and new developments happened. The reason is that the people in every age with reference to the problems they faced in their day-to-day lives discarded certain past practices in order to introduce changes for further growth and progress which would avert revolution. In the light of this it is worthwhile to note what happened in the past either from very ancient times or during the immediate past as dealt with by

Dr. R. Thiyagarajan and Thiru B.P. Chandramohan. However, the merits of such things are not discussed in this foreword.

Consumerism is a concept which deals with the activity of selling and buying of usable non-perishable and keepable articles and cosumable and perishable goods. How and in what manner such transactions in these goods are carried out by the producers, marketers, wholesale traders and the retail traders are certain matters of importance. Why the users, namely the consumers buy the goods, use them for their needs, how do they find those goods, whether they are good or bad, whether they are according to tested and approved standards and whether they aid and assist the consumers in enjoying and making use of them constitute the other and important basic issues which needed to be considered. Further in this process all forces of capital, production, labour and distribution play a vital and significant role. Here, the consumers are parties who have to be aware clearly of the norms, ethics and methods followed by the agents of production and distribution. The government has a duty to aid and advice the consumers and oversees all these activities in order to make sure that every thing went right. Where there are lapses it has to intervene and take action for remedying them.

It is a well known fact that consumerism as it is understood today could not have been there in India in the past and is comparatively a late 20th Century phenomenon taking root more or less in the last two decades only preceding the 21st Century. It is pertinent to note the authors' reference to Justice Thiru K. Sampath, President of State Consumer Disputes Redressal Commission, Government of Tamilnadu pointing to pre- and post-Independence enactments in this regard. These acts cover such aspects and areas as contract goods, agricultural produce, drugs, food adulteration, service maintenance, black marketing and standards to mention the very important among many. A cursory glance of the items included in the list above makes it clear and beyond doubt that there are present issues which very much affect the consumers in every way. When allowed such issues and practices thereon to happen un-checked and un-regulated could wreck havoc on the health and spell ruin to the social and economic fabric of the society. Further they could affect the activities of not only the enlightened and particularly the un-enlightened consumers needed no emphasis. Let us ask the question. Who among the educated for example the academicians, officials in government departments, private agencies/private organizations various service institutions do really know and among who know a little take care to devote time, energy and money for bringing to notice of the authorities and all concerned the failures, mal-practices, defects and the several such things for redressal? If it is really done by a handful or a few was ever action initiated? If so how and in what manner? With what result? Has there been a machinery to follow them up and monitor the outcome? Was ever any attempt made to assess the impact of these on the consumers? Were the verdicts of courts dealing with consumer issues followed? Answers to these and other similar questions could explain the successes and failures of consumer movements.

This book in this regard brings home the point that "One cannot get the benefits by just claiming the rights alone" and that the "beneficiaries have to perform certain responsibilities". They should involve actively, work together, organize themselves and be ready to fight injustice whereever necessary. The authors explain clearly the meaning and import of consumer service and its various facets. Under Consumer Protection Act of 1986 'service' meant service of any description which is made available to potential users and included the provision of facilities in connection with banking, insurance, transport, processing, supply of electrical or other energy, boarding or lodging or both, housing, construction, entertainment or amusement and providing news or other information and the likes. In this context it is of importance to note that service here meant service for which a fee is paid by the consumer or fee collected by those who rendered service, e.g. doctor, lawyer, teacher, manufacturer, trader and merchant. It included also services such as transport, retail and whole- sale trade, sports, government administration, defence and community services. Thus, the service sector by its very nature consisted of a heterogeneous set of activities. In short they could be grouped under professional services, business services, industrial services, producer services, distribution services and the social services.

Consumers have the rights to get quality and standard goods. Similarly they are entitled to reasonable, timely and efficient services at competitive prices. They further have rights to be protected against substandard goods, to get information about quality, purity, standard and prices of goods. Finally, they have the right to get redressal against malpractices of merchants, traders, suppliers and manufacturers of goods. It is indeed interesting that the chief editor has stated that the consumers are at the top and they are accorded the status of a Monarch by calling them as 'the Kings'. This should make clear to all how much of importance the consumers enjoyed under the laws.

Inspite of all these as pointed out by a contributor consumerism is in its infancy only and it is slowly developing in India. The reason according to him, for this, is mainly the apathy of consumers. It is partly only true. but many of them are not aware of the laws enacted in this respect could be correct. To illustrate this take the situation that is present in fields like education, health care, manufacture of medicines and their sale, hospital services, sports activities, welfare programmes of government, transport systems, insurance, tax collection, administration of public corporations and services of similar bodies. The consumers no doubt are benefited in several ways with the enforcement of the consumer laws but much more remained to be achieved for greater and better services. However, it cannot be refuted that the consumers' interests yet are not fully taken care of and that generally in every field of activity there are present serious lapses and deficiencies. The road to achieve optimum success is long and unending as of now.

As the proverbial saying went that the test of a single particle of the whole is enough to prove the quality of and ready to the eatability of a cooked pudding. Take the case of the medical sector in India. Even in the case where there is fee structure for different kinds of services and treatment the cost of it is exorbitant and in a majority of instances it is prohibitive. For this trend the blame could be put partly on public health services and agencies. These are limited and could not deliver the services to the required levels. Another reason is that the population increased in enormous proportions while the resources available to public bodies to maintain the health services do not increase to that level. Therefore, it led the private to exploit the unfortunate poor sections both urban and rural. The lot of the rural is greater. It is detrimental to the well being of the masses of the society. Where has gone the spirit of service and rendering of treatment to mitigation of pain and distress of the needy poor, helpless, the infirm and the aged.

Another area of concern is the pharmaceuticals and pharmacies. These do not certainly follow or adhere to the laws and the ethics of business. Take the matter of selling and buying of medicines. Here certain procedures and practices of the drug manufacturing companies and the public and private agencies are not certainly good. For example inviting quotations and giving orders to supply to those who give the lowest rates is not a good practice to follow in this sector. In this method the medicines supplied are of sub-standard which could lead to dangerous situations for both the medical practioners and patients. Similarly some doctors have understanding with the drug suppliers who want to get higher profit manufacture duplicate medicines which would be available in shops with which doctors have understanding only. Further a vast majority of medical shops do not give bills for medicines bought though they collect taxes. What percentage of taxes is collected none knows and usually a larger amount alone is collected. The consumers are taken for a ride by them. As medicine have become a daily necessity people by them paying higher price. Yet another practice is printing the MRP. The amount mentioned in several cases is several times higher than the manufacturing cost thus enabling the medical shop owners to get 100 per cent and more profit. For instance take a disposable syringe which costs Rs. 1.50 per piece is priced at Rs. 4.90. Another undesirable practice is printing of the price in fractions of paise 02 or 99. How do they calculate the tax? All these give room for very unfair trade practices which go against interests of the sick patients and consumers.

The spirit of philanthropy and public good which were the considerations in the past has all been given a go by people these days. Self interest and greed rule the roost now. What are at the bottom of these evils are the declining standards of service in almost in every sector. The education sector is far worse than the other worst sectors. The system that is in practice is one which permitted commercialization of it. Appointment to faculty positions, admission of students into various courses and prescription of fee are not with reference to the value of the courses and the probable expenditure to be incurred but on considerations of filling the coffers of the managements offering education. Even millionaires wanted to amass wealth throwing justice, fairplay decency to the winds, no, no, to the gutters. What is the situation in the medical and other professional courses? It is all money, money and money alone. The government for its part instead of curtailing such trends encouraged them. The sector which should set an example and be a model itself has decayed is something unpardonable Education is the basis of every thing. Therefore, this sector needed immediate cleansing of all its evils and crimes. If this is done other things will follow automatically. There is no end to this kind of references and what has been pointed out is more than sufficient to invite the attention of consumers to the present state of affairs of the consumer sector.

Inspite of all these there is a silver lining yet. There are some individuals and institutions which do service still as ordained by the scriptures, ethical laws and the like. The government also should try to take suitable steps to prevent the private agencies from becoming Midas like and indulge in unrestricted exploitation of the consumers and enable the consumers to enjoy the fruits and the benefits that accrue by the steps taken by the institutions created under the consumer laws. A word of caution. These days in order to overcome the failure of public bodies of the Government often some people suggest privatization of every thing. This is not a desirable move and it should be resisted. But insist on taking corrective steps and extend full support to the government. Dr. V.N. Viswanathan is a great scholar in his own merit and he has to his credit several publications the academics, the students and the enlightened public holds him in high esteem for his achievements. I am proud of him. I congratulate him for bringing out this volume in the service of the consumers.

DR. S. SUBRAMANIAN
Vice-President and Executive Council Member,
Indian Institute of Public Administration, New Delhi,
Former Professor and Head,
Department of Political Science,
Madurai Kamaraj University

Preface

This book helps you understand the everyday transactions in the service sector, and sets out the basic rights and obligations of people extending service for consideration. When you are better informed, your choices will be greater and you'll get the genuine things for your money. It deals with the consumer laws in India and the various means of protecting the interests of the consumers. In the international conference on consumer protection held in Malaysia in 1997, the Indian Consumer Protection Act was described as one "which has set in motion a revolution in the fields of consumer rights, the parallel of which has not been seen anywhere else in the world." But despite such appreciation there are grey areas in consumer protection laws and welfare particularly in the service areas by the service providers. 'Service Deficiency' is the focal point taken for discussions and the remedial measures are presented for various services through redressal mechanisms of particular service providers and by consumer courts at district, state and national level.

Consumers have sought protection through legislation because the general laws and market forces have failed to provide it. Many consumer protection laws either relate to the terms and conditions of contracts that consumers make with suppliers for the supply of goods and services, or to encourage the making of such contracts (marketing, packaging, advertising and provision of information). Parallel laws, especially the law of contracts, assumed that the parties to contracts are *legally* equal in terms of power and information. In substance, in real markets, almost invariably consumers have markedly less power and information than suppliers. The law deems the action of a consumer in buying a commodity to be the making of a contract—in theory a free, consensual act. In practice, the legal consequences are attributed to the action by the law without any consideration of what the consumer actually knows or wants. The common law of contracts simply cannot afford consumers the protection they probably would seek if they were rational, fully informed, and equal in economic power to the supplier. Because contract law offers an inadequate basis for an equitable legal transaction, it must be modified by legislation in order to afford greater protection to consumers than they can negotiate individually for themselves.

The book is written in a simple and lucid style from multi-disciplinary perspectives. It will be a useful source of information for the Indian consumers, lawyers, members of voluntary organizations, officials of the government, research institutions and college students. It is a collection of papers presented by reputed scholars, lawyers, academicians, and government officials focusing on different service areas of consumer interests.

31.01.2007
Chennai.

V.N. Viswanathan

Acknowledgements

I owe my acknowledgements for many who directly and indirectly helped me in conceiving the idea of consumer rights in service sector. I am greatly indebted to Professor S.S. Singh, Professor of Justice and Administration, Indian Institute of Public Administration, New Delhi for his invitation to partake in the national level workshop (August 4–8, 2005) where we had exceptional discussions on several issues of consumer rights. I must also thank Dr. P.L. Sanjeev Reddy, Director of Indian Institute of Public Administration for introducing national level authorities, judges and officials who involved themselves in various activities of consumer forums. Secondly, I extend my sincere thanks to the Ministry of Food, Public Distribution and Consumer Affairs for the sanctioning of the project on consumer festivals for colleges and universities. My experiences in conducting several programmes of consumer festivals gave me first hand knowledge of consumer related issues and I was able to establish contacts with officials and members of NGOs, members of consumer courts and benefited to a large extent. The Principals of the premier educational institution in India, Presidency College were very cooperative and encouraged me in awareness creating programmes. For free and frank discussion my friend S.K. Kamat DCT's Dhempe College of Arts and Science, Miramar, Goa has been instrumental for the publication of this book. In the Department of Political Science, all my colleagues extended a whole hearted cooperation in conducting the seminar and I must mention the encouragement shown by the head of the department Dr. M. Kaliyaperumal and M. Murali, Selection Grade Lecturer of the political science department.

On several occasions I got encouragement from my mentor teacher Dr. S. Subramanian, Vice-President of Indian Institute of Public Administration, New Delhi and former head of the department, Department of Political Science, Madurai Kamaraj University,

Madurai. His intellectual guidance has led me to conduct the state level seminar successfully. My research scholar Mr. D.S. Makkalanban joined me in editing this volume and also involved in data-entry of all the papers presented in the seminar. Within a short notice of time several leading academician, government officials, judicial members and members from consumer related NGOs participated and presented papers. They gave life to this book and sustained the knowledge on consumer related matters. My special thanks to Justice K. Sampath, President, State Consumer Disputes Redressal Commission, Government of Tamil Nadu whose valedictory address and paper presentation widened our knowledge on the actual working of the consumer courts. Officials from the Department of Public Distribution and Consumer Protection, Government of Tamil Nadu helped us in the establishment of consumer club in college. The Chairmen of the two panels constituted for the seminar Dr. K. Jayaraman and Dr. A. Ravishankar conducted the seminar smoothly and gave opportunity for a lively discussion on several issues.

V.N. VISWANATHAN

Contents

PART III
SERVICES IN HEALTH

PART IV
SERVICES IN TRANSPORT

PART V
SERVICES IN INSURANCE

PART VI
CONSUMER RIGHTS AND THEIR PROTECTION

Appendices

Appendices

List of Abbreviations

AIIMS	All India Institute of Medical Sciences
BIS	Bureau of Indian Standards
CCC	Consumer Coordination Council
CCEC	Consumer Council Executive Committee
CCIL	Coca-Cola India Ltd
CMC	Christian Medical College
COBO	Company Owned Bottling Operations
CPA	Consumer Protection Act
CWF	Consumer Welfare Fund
ECA	Essential Commodities Act
FAO	Food and Agriculture Organization
FCI	Food Corporation of India
FEDCOT	Federation of Consumer Organization of Tamil Nadu
FIPB	Foreign Investment Promotion Board
FOBO	Franchisee Owned Bottling Operations
GATS	General Agreement on Trade in Services
GDP	Gross Domestic Product
GIC	General Insurance Corporation of India
IIPA	Indian Institute of Public Administration
IMA	Indian Medical Association
IMC	Indian Medical Council
IRA	Insurance Regulatory Authority
IRDA	Insurance Regulatory and Development Authority
LIC	Life Insurance Corporation of India
MMPO	Milk and Milk Products Order
MoU	Memorandum of Understanding
MP	Madhya Pradesh
MRP	Maximum Retail Price
MRTP	Monopolies and Restrictive Trade Practices Act

MSP	Minimum Support Price
MTNL	Mahanagar Telephone Nigam Limted
NCDRC	National Consumer Dispute Redressal Commission
NEME	North East Europe/Middle East Group
NGO	Non-Governmental Organization
NRI	Non-Resident Indian
OP	Opposite Party
PAIC	Punjab Agro Industries Corporation
PDS	Public Distribution System
QOS	Quality of Service
SBI	State Bank of India
TTE	Travelling Ticket Examiner
UGC	University Grants Commission
UK	United Kingdom
UN	United Nations
UNESCO	United Nations Economic and Social Council
UTP	Unfair Trade Practice
WHO	World Health Organization
WMA	Weights and Measures Act

List of Contributors

Dr. A. Sethuramasubbiah, Faculty, Tamil Nadu Institute of Labour Studies, Chennai-600005.

Dr. B.P. Chandramohan, Reader, Department of Economics, Presidency College (Autonomous), Chennai-600005.

Mr. C.M.K. Thampi, S.S.L. in Economics, Department of Economics, Presidency College, Chennai-600005.

Dr. D. Rudrappan, Head of the Department, Department of Post-Graduate and Research Studies in Economics, Presidency College, Chennai-600005.

Mr. D.S. Makkalanban, Research Scholar, Department of Political Science, Presidency College, Chennai-600005.

Hon'ble Justice K. Sampath, President, Tamil Nadu State Consumer Disputes Redressal Commission, Chennai, Tamil Nadu, India.

Tmt. Mythili K. Rajendran, Deputy Commissioner (City North), Civil Supplies and Consumer Protection Department, Ezhilagam, Chennai-600005.

Tmt. P. Brinda, Lecturer, Tamil Nadu Dr. Ambedkar Law University, Chennai.

Mr. R. Elangovan, Ph.D. Research Scholar, Department of Political Science, Presidency College, Chennai-600005.

Dr. R. Thiagarajan, Head of the Department, Department of Sanskrit, Presidency College, Chennai-600005.

Tmt. S. Ganga Bai, Deputy Commissioner (City South), Civil Supplies and Consumer Protection Department, Ezhilagam, Chennai-600005.

Dr. S. Marcelin Pushpa, Lecturer, Department of Public Administration, Anna Adarsh College for Women, Chennai.

Dr. S. Ravishankar, Reader, Anna Centre for Public Affairs, University of Madras, Chennai-600005.

Tmt. S.S. Pankajam, Lecturer, Department of English (Evening), Ethiraj College for Women, Chennai.

Mr. T.G. Ethirajulu, LIC Agent, Chennai.

Dr. V.N. Viswanathan (Editor), Reader in Political Science, Presidency College, Chennai.

Introduction

Consumer Rights in Service Sector

V.N. VISWANATHAN

'Rights' based issues are not only occupying the public space in the last two decades in India but also the academic world particularly this is very much true with issues of human rights, consumer rights and right to information. The Government of India legislated first in the field of consumer rights in the year 1986, second came the Human Rights Protection Act 1993 and third is the Right to Information Act in 2005. These three acts are considered an epoch making an historical milestone in the annals of India's political development. A vibrant democracy must necessarily make people to participate in the process of governing by enjoying certain rights. From a common man's point of view, the day-to-day life is much governed by seller and buyer relationships and thus making consumer rights as more popular rights. In the context of privatization and liberalization the market is flooded with numerous products and hitherto unknown services. The Ministry of Consumer Affairs, Food and Public Distribution making all possible efforts in creating awareness about the consumer rights and the working of various redressal forums in our nation. 'Consumer Education' is one of the established goals of the Ministry of Food, Public Distribution and Consumer Affairs. Such awareness is made through consumer festivals in colleges, and financing consumer related project by the Ministry through Indian Institute of Public Administration (IIPA, New Delhi). Infact, my own interest in the field of consumer rights arise as a result of my participation in a workshop conducted by IIPA during August 4–8, 2005. By sanctioning of a project under the scheme of Consumer Festivals in Colleges, I was involved in a series of consumer awareness activities conducted through Presidency College, Chennai. The project involves creating consumer awareness among college students in Chennai city. The major activities were:

1. Celebrating consumer day.
2. Visiting Consumer Redressal Forums.
3. Conducting quiz programme for college students on consumer welfare.
4. Issuing of handouts on consumer rights to the public.
5. Conducting various inter-collegiate competitions.
6. Conducting State level seminars and inviting speakers from State Consumer Disputes Redressal Commission/State Departments/Consumer Welfare Associations.
7. Establishment of Consumer Club and thus involving the students in understanding consumer related issues.
8. Television and radio presentations on consumer rights and welfare.
9. Encouraging research on consumer related issues.
10. Coordinating with other colleges in order to develop consumer welfare curriculum as an optional paper.

My involvement as a project coordinator gave me first hand information on consumer related issues and the mechanisms to redress the felt difficulties of the consumers by consumer forums. This provided me an opportunity to join with many non-governmental agencies involved themselves with consumer welfare such as FEDCOT, Civic Action Group, VOICE, and Consumer Educational organizations. As a part of the consumer festival a State level seminar was conducted on 16th October, 2006 at Presidency College and it was overwhelmingly responded by academicians, government officials, non-governmental organizations, research scholars, students and the public. The major focus of the seminar was to highlight the ways and means to redress the deficiency in service sector through various redressal forums and thus protecting the interest and welfare of the consumers. Besides this, the seminar also focused on creating awareness both for students and the public.

Conceptual Framework of the Seminar

The Consumer Protection Act, 1986 is an epoch making enactment, which protect the interest of the consumers. The Act ensures the maintenance of satisfactory standards in the market relating to goods and services. In the context of consumer welfare only goods (product) related consumer disputes that are prominently attracted the media and the academic attention. This altogether has led to shadowing of "service" related matters to the understanding of common man. The economic globalization and privatization in India calls for a review of service sector. Developmental politics necessitates an ever-expanding scope for protecting the interest of the ordinary consumers and creating a knowledge society. As a consequence, the situation warrants for a more transparent and easy access to redressal forums for resolving service related consumer problems. Besides, evolving of internal mechanisms for the redressal of deficiency in service by various service providers such as Banking Ombudsman and Telephone Adalath, the external regulatory authorities must also tuned with the development new issues. The Consumer Forums must also expand its scope to provide relief to the growing new services (such as Internet) in the event of gross deficiency in service.

The ever growing nature of service sector in the Indian economy caution us the need for effective regulatory agencies by various service providers like banking, insurance, telecommunication, postal service, transport, power supply service, house construction and the health care service. The existing inbuilt setup must be overhauled to cope with consumer protection laws and welfare. The seminar highlights that there exist a substantial differences in remedies available for deficiency in service in relation to goods (products) and for a deficient service. Papers are invited on the above-described conceptual framework of specific service area and the new challenges faced by the consumers. Papers must be an eye-opener for the ordinary consumers in India who face the ordeal of deficiency in service in the background of a much complex technical advancement of various services. The role of Consumer Redressal institutions, professional bodies and NGOs are significant in resolving service related issues faced by the consumers.

The service sector consists of the "soft" parts of the economy such as insurance, tourism, banking, retail and education. In soft sector employment, people use time to deploy knowledge assets, collaboration assets, and process-engagement to create productivity (effectiveness), performance improvement potential (potential) and sustainability. Typically the output of this time is content (information), service, attention, advice, experiences, and/or discussion (*aka*, "intangible goods"). Other examples of service sector employment include:

- Franchising,
- Restaurants,
- Retailing,
- Entertainment, including the Record industry, Music industry, Radio, Television and Movies,
- News media,
- Leisure industry,
- Consulting,
- Transport,
- Healthcare, and
- Consulting, Investment and Legal advice and services.

All complaints related to deficiency in service in electricity supply, drinking water supply, telecommunication, railways, banks, insurance companies, etc., can be filed in the district forum.

The need to recognize and enforce the rights of consumers is being understood and several laws have been made for this purpose. In India, we have the Indian Contract Act, the Sale of Goods Act, the Dangerous Drugs Act, the Agricultural Produce (Grading and Marketing) Act, the Indian Standards Institution (Certification Marks) Act, the Prevention of Food Adulteration Act, the Standards of Weights and Measures Act, the Trade and Merchandise Marks Act, etc. which to some extent protect consumer interests. However, these laws required the consumer to initiate action by way of a civil suit which involved lengthy legal process proving to be too expensive and time consuming for lay consumers. Therefore, the need for a simpler and quicker access to redressal to consumer grievances was felt and accordingly, it lead to the legislation of the Consumer Protection Act, 1986.

The Consumer Protection Act, 1986 provides that if there is a deficiency in the goods or services provided to a consumer for which he has paid, he can file a complaint at a district forum (for claims up to Rs. 25 lakh), a state commission (up to Rs. 1 crore), or the National Consumer Dispute Redressal Commission (NCDRC; for claims above Rs. 1 crore).

Accordingly, papers are invited from faculty members, research scholars, and service area specialist, members of NGO's and from lawyers. Practicing lawyers were encouraged to present case laws relating to redressal of deficiency in services from various fields.

The book is an outcome of the proceedings of the seminar. Understandably, if one reads the literature on consumer rights, one can find more issues to product related issues than consumer rights in service sector. Leading economists of India are of the view that India is poised for a phenomenal growth in the service sector by the end of 2010. The service sector contribution to national GDP which stood as 21 per cent in 1951 today almost touched 50 per cent of the national GDP. India is a leading service provider not only within the nation but also to other nations. The 'new economy' fostered a new responsibility in providing service of international standard by various service providers. The introduction of mobile phone and internet services created a totally different atmosphere in getting access to services as well to remedial measures in case of drastic deficiency in services. Again, in the context of shrinking role of Government, there has been a growth of NGOs which will take the role of monitoring agencies and report things to regulatory agencies or the Government. Becoming a member in consumer NGOs ensures a direct participation of the public in the governing process. Such sense of participation will further enhance our democratic credentials. As stated by Lucian Pye, the grass-root participation in the governing process will lead to stronger democracy. Consumer welfare associations in India thus facilitate grass-root participation and also make a vigil over unethical practices of sellers market. Here, the consumer associations act as a watch dog over the market economy which quite often favours the producers and the sellers than the consumers.

The need for consumer education and empowerment are becoming the clarion call in almost all the nations. Consumers cannot be cheated and ruthlessly exploited by the sellers and the service providers. The Department of Consumer Affairs under Ministry of Food and Consumer Affairs is responsible for the formulation of policies for Consumer Cooperatives, Monitoring Prices, and availability of essential commodities, Consumer Movement in the country and Controlling of statutory bodies like Bureau of Indian Standards (BIS) and Weights and Measures.[1] There are certain universal consumer rights which are recognized by the Government of India which are as follows:

Right to Safety

Means right to be protected against the marketing of goods and services, which are hazardous to life and property. The purchased goods and services availed of should not only meet their immediate needs, but also fulfil long-Term interests.

Right to Information

Means right to be informed about the quality, quantity, potency, purity, standard and price of goods so as to protect the consumer against unfair trade practices.

Right to Choose

Means right to be assured, wherever possible of access to variety of goods and services at competitive price. In case of monopolies, it means right to be assured of satisfactory quality and service at a fair price. It also includes right to basic goods and services. This is because unrestricted right of the minority to choose can mean a denial for the majority of its fair share. This right can be better exercised in a competitive market where a variety of goods are available at competitive prices.

Right to be Heard

Means that consumer's interests will receive due consideration at appropriate forums. It also includes right to be represented in various forums formed to consider the consumer's welfare.

The Consumers should form non-political and non-commercial consumer organizations which can be given representation in various committees formed by the Government and other bodies in matters relating to consumers.

Right to Seek Redressal

Means right to seek redressal against unfair trade practices or unscrupulous exploitation of consumers. It also includes right to fair settlement of the genuine grievances of the consumer.

Consumers must make complaint for their genuine grievances. Many a times their complaint may be of small value but its impact on the society as a whole may be very large. They can also take the help of consumer organizations in seeking redressal of their grievances.

Right to Consumer Education

Means the right to acquire the knowledge and skill to be an informed consumer throughout life. Ignorance of consumers, particularly of rural consumers, is mainly responsible for their exploitation. They should know their rights and must exercise them. Only then real consumer protection can be achieved with success.

The U.N. guidelines for consumer protection are meant to achieve the following objectives:

(a) to assist countries in achieving or maintaining adequate protection for their population as consumers;
(b) to facilitate production and distribution patterns responsive to the needs and desires of consumers;
(c) to encourage high levels of ethical conduct for those engaged in the production and distribution of goods and services to consumers;
(d) to assist countries in curbing abusive business practices by all enterprises at the national and international levels which adversely affect consumers;
(e) to facilitate the development of independent consumer groups;
(f) to further the international cooperation in the field of consumer protection; and
(g) to encourage the development of market conditions which provide consumers with greater choice at lower prices.

It is interesting to note that in spite of U.N. recognition, encouragement from the developed countries and the pro-active role played by the Government, the consumer in India still does not get his due. It is time that he wakes up and realizes his rights. It will be useful if voluntary consumer organizations take up this role and make way for the realizations of the objectives of the U.N. guidelines and the Consumer Protection Act.

Consumer Disputes Redressal Agencies in India

There shall be established for the purposes of this Act, the following agencies, namely:

(a) A Consumer Disputes Redressal Forum to be known as the 'District Forum' established by the State Government in each district of the State by notification: Provided that the State Government may, if it deems fit, establish more than one District Forum in a district;
(b) A Consumer Disputes Redressal Commission to be known as the 'State Commission' established by the State Government in the State by notification; and
(c) A National Consumer Disputes Redressal Commission established by the Central Government by notification.

Consumer protection law or consumer law is considered an area of public law that regulates private law relationships between individual consumers and the businesses that sell them goods and services. Consumer protection covers a wide range of topics including but not necessarily limited to product liability, privacy rights, unfair business practices, fraud, misrepresentation, and other consumer/business interactions. Under Consumer Protection Act of 1986 'service' means service of any description which is made available to potential users and includes, but not limited to, the provision of facilities in connection with banking, financing insurance, transport, processing, supply of electrical or other energy, board or lodging or both, housing construction, entertainment, amusement or the purveying of news or other information, but does not include the rendering of any service free of charge or under a contract of personal service.

'Service' can be generally defined as acts provided in return for payment. Repairing a car is a service rendered for money. Service occupations—occupations in which the task is providing a service (doctor, lawyer, wait person, teacher). In all economies, the service sector by its very nature comprises a very heterogeneous set of activities. It is made of financial and telecom services, of restaurants and hotels, transport, retail and wholesale trade, sports and entertainment, government administration and defence, and personal and community (NGO) services. There is an additional dimension to the service sector in India. There is heterogeneity here in the drivers of expansion of services. There is the traditional source of growth—the development of industry leading to the development of services such as transport, trade and the like. The need for empowering consumer organizations with proper training on regulatory issues and regulatory basics has to be recognized. Their involvement in such process would make qualitative changes in regulatory governance.

There are different types of services such as:

- *Professional Services*: Provide knowledge based services that enhance the well-being of individuals of firms who are clients.
- *Business Services:* Assist firms and organizations in carrying out their economic functions temporary help industry
- *Producer Services:* Provide services necessary to help other industries create their products of services.
- *Distributive Services:* Provide services that disperse goods geographically.
- *Social Services:* Services provided to benefit society as a whole.
- *Personal Services:* Produced principally for families and individuals.

What factors might we identify that lead to service sector growth? The supply has increased because the demand has increased

1. Services arise from new manufactured products.
2. Services grow when market production replaces home production.
3. Services grow when consumers have more disposable income.
4. Demand for services is insatiable most services not like manufactured goods.
5. Expansion of local and state government and social services.
6. Expansion of health care (hospitals, retirement homes, etc).
7. Information-based economy and business services.

Quality of Service—Definitional Issues

What would constitute 'quality of service' would depend on the sector under consideration. Also, parameters that measure quality in a given sector vary across countries. For example, development indicators (such as telephone density) are not QOS (quality of service) indicators in UK, while they are in India. In UK's electricity sector, 'keeping appointment' with the utility is one of the indicators, but it is not in India. Typically, a network industry such as telecommunication or electricity industry is expected to ensure high quality of service, if combination of network quality and service quality to its customer improves, the former being the core of the overall quality of service. The quality of service should not be static, rather dynamic. Thus, depending on the stages of development in a particular sector, the parameters governing quality of service in a given sector could vary over time.

Therefore, the following regulatory issues are required to be addressed:

(a) What should be the regulator's role in ensuring Quality of Service (QOS)?
(b) How does one define 'QOS' in a sector?
(c) Would there be any need to provide uniformity on certain QOS parameters across sectors? For example 'keeping appointments' might be a generic QOS indicator, which could be made applicable across all sectors.
(d) Should the different QOS parameters be static; and if not, how should they be made dynamic?

Since consumer is the "king" in the new style of governance, the interests of the consumer would have to be protected, and he has to be provided with a quality service at reasonable costs. Further, his complaints as regards poor quality of services must be quickly redressed. Even before the introduction of regulatory legislation in sectors such as electricity, telecom, or ports, the Consumer Protection Act (CPA), 1986, sought to promote and protect the following rights of the consumers:

(a) The right to be protected against marketing of goods and services which are hazardous to life and property;
(b) The right to be informed about quality, purity, standard and price of goods or services as the case may be, so as to protect the consumer against unfair trade practices;

(c) The right to be assured, whenever, possible, access to a variety of goods and services at competitive prices;

(d) The right to be heard, and to be assured that consumer's interests will receive due consideration at appropriate forum.

A complaint under the Act also includes an allegation relating to "the services hired or availed of or agreed to be hired or availed by him suffer from one or more defects". Further, a "deficiency" is defined as "any fault, imperfection, shortcoming or inadequacy in the quality, nature and manner of performance which is required be maintained by or under any law for the time being in force or has been undertaken to be performed by a person in pursuance of a contract or otherwise in relation to any service". Section 2 defines the "service" as "any description which is made available to potential users and includes the provision of facilities in connection with banking, financing, insurance, transport, processing, supply of electrical energy or other energy, board, or lodging,...., but does not include the rendering of any service free of charge or under a contract of "personal service". To address the consumer grievances under the Act, there are consumer fora in various states as well at the national level.

From consumer perspective a host of issues were brought under discussion in the seminar and people were invited from different disciplines in order to cope up with the inter-disciplinary nature of the issues itself.

The first chapter of this book is written by Han'ble Justice K. Sampath, President of State Consumer Disputes Redressal Commission, and Government of Tamil Nadu. He presented the whole issues of consumer rights tracing from its historical settings and the legal mechanisms to redress the consumer disputes and the role of legal institutions connected with it. He adds further that we have both pre-independence and post-independence laws enacted. Some of them are:

1. Indian Contract Act, 1872
2. Sale of Goods Act, 1930
3. Agricultural Produce (Grading and Marketing) Act, 1937
4. Drugs and Cosmetics Act, 1940
5. Drugs (Control) Act, 1950

6. Drugs and Magic Remedies (Objectionable Advertisements) Act, 1954
7. Prevention of Food Adulteration Act, 1954; Essential Commodities Act, 1955
8. Standards of Weights and Measures Act, 1956
9. Trade and Merchandise Marks Act, 1958
10. Essential Services Maintenance Act, 1968
11. The Monopolies and Restrictive Trade Practices Act, 1969
12. Prevention of Black Marketing and Maintenance of Supplies of Essential Commodities Act, 1980
13. Bureau of Indian Standards Act, 1986.

He widely covers the service sectors like banking, builders-promoters, courier services, educational service, electricity, health care service, insurance and school services with suitable case laws. One cannot get the benefits by just claiming the rights alone and he emphasizes that there are certain responsibilities for the consumers in order to enjoy these rights.

Consumer Responsibilities

(a) Critical awareness and vigilance,
(b) Involvement and being alert and active,
(c) To practice sustainable consumption—Social concern,
(d) Concern for the environment—to be responsible to the environment, and
(e) Working together—to be organized and fight for justice.

The second chapter written by Dr. R. Thiagarajan takes us to ancient India where once upon a time all modern consumer rights were prevailed and the King guarded those rights for the benefits of his citizens. He traced the roots of present Consumer Protection Act from the four important Hindu laws such as DHARMA, VYAVAHARA, CARITRA, and RAJASASANA. As India's leading Sanskrit scholar, he presented very interesting facts such as the practice of giving receipt for the transactions, the do's and don'ts of business in ancient period. It is true that the ancient practices were the prelude for the present laws of consumer protection. The present day practice of identifying quality of product by gold mark, wool mark, ISI, AGMARK were also advocated in ancient India by Sage Yajnavalkya for gold, zari, tin and bronze.

In chapter three, B.P. Chandramohan's paper examines various difficulties in the compliance of traditional control, regulations and licenses in terms of time and resources, possibilities of corruption and malpractices. Too many controls and regulations will instigate inefficiency of trading practices and ultimately reduce the consumers' welfare he opined. He tries to give a sellers point of view and says that multi-level regulatory authorities will hamper the producer's enthusiasms of production and this also true with service sector. He presents that there are at present more than 400 laws that govern the trade. Some of the laws outlived their utility and appear arbitrary and will take the competition spirit from the traders. Though there are hundreds of such legislations, the consumers are seldom protected from adulteration, exploitation or cheat but the trading activity has been seriously affected due to unnecessary interventions, harassment and corruptions of the officials in the bottom rungs of administration. It is altogether a different vision that one should not treat in a light manner.

In chapter four, A. Sethuramasubbiah laments that consumerism has not taken a firm root in India as in western societies. He cited various case laws in the field of service sector and concludes that there is further need of awareness which can be fulfilled by the student's community in India.

In chapter five, Thampi proclaims that in the early law, the doctrine of "Caveat Emptor"—"let the buyer beware" was the philosophy of law of sales. Today it has been replaced by "Caveat Venditor"—"Let the seller beware". So today, the buyers are more protected from unethical business practices. The author draws the parallel between MRTP Act and the CP Act, 1986. It is interesting to note that both laws and its instructions are running parallel to give protection to consumers. He presented many case laws to prove his point of argument, particularly with reference to unfair trade practices and misleading advertisements. The author adds that consumerism is in its infancy in India. It is slowly developing. Apathy of consumers has slackened the growth of consumerism. Many consumers just do not know the legislations available in our country. For instance vegetable oil should be sold in kilograms. Selling the same in liters is an offence.

In chapter six, D. Rudrappan discusses the status of higher education in India. He says that National Commission established under the Act is yet to examine the question, whether educational services come under the purview of consumer courts. Meanwhile, Calcutta and Madras High Courts have categorically held that educational institutions do not come under the ambit of consumer courts. In this scenario, Ministry of Consumer Affairs Government of India has incorporated certain amendments to this act removing the deficiency relating to service sector. Dwelling at length on the present predicament and the persisting challenges of higher education, the paper has hinted at the dwindling financial support by the government and consequent drive for commercialization of higher education by educational barrens besides emphasizing on protection of consumers in higher education and the available mechanism for redressal of deficiency of educational service in terms of Competition Act, 2002.

In chapter seven, Marcelin S. Pushpa focused on health care sector and cited many case laws that paid compensation for medical negligence. She examined the procedures that had been adopted at health care facilities to respond to consumers' concerns and complaints. It also assessed the utility and effectiveness of different forums established under the Consumer Protection Act to pay compensation to aggrieved consumers for deliberate acts of negligence that had caused loss or damage to the patient. It took into consideration the perspectives of the consumers, the providers, and the law and reviewed the outcomes of medical negligence cases in legal and statutory (medical councils) systems. In her concluding passage she says that every citizen should have access to high-quality health care services and be able to claim compensation for deliberate acts of negligence or for unfair trade practices. The laws should also cover doctors working in government hospitals and charitable institutions.

In chapter eight, P. Brinda focused on 'Medical Negligence'. It means lack of reasonable care, skill or willful negligence on part of a doctor in respect of acceptance of a patient, while taking history, while examining, while carrying out diagnosis or investigations, or even while treating either medically or surgically, etc. which may cause or result in some kind of injury or damage to or death of the patient. Two basic propositions laid down in law regarding liability for negligence are: firstly, "Breach of Duty" to care and secondly, standard of care, i.e. the practitioner must bring to his task a reasonable degree of skill, knowledge and exercise a reasonable degree of care with caution (neither the very highest, nor a very low degree of care).

The most important contribution of P. Brinda is the concept of 'informed consent' that a doctor must get from the patient. The Indian Medical Association had campaigned against the inclusion ofmedical services under the Consumer Protection Act on the grounds that medical services could not be equated with consumer transactions involving ordinary products and services. But in many cases cited by her compensations were awarded for medical negligence and deficiency in services.

In chapter nine, D.S. Makkalanban presented a paper on service in the railway sector and the various mechanisms available to mitigate the problems faced by the consumers as railway travelers. He points out that Section 3 of the Consumer Protection Act is considered by many scholars of consumer law as being the strongest and most effective section. Further, since Consumer Dispute Redressal Fora are established in every single district in this country under this law, Section 3 allows millions of consumers to access justice at their own districts—an accomplishment unmatched by any law. It is significant to concede that effort was made by a part of sellers and service providers to pull down Section 3 a few years ago, but the Indian Parliament did not allow this to happen. He highlighted the warpath between the Railway Tribunal and the Consumer Fora in awarding compensation for deficiency in service by the railway authorities.

In chapter ten, T.G. Ethirajulu provided a practical guidance to the insurance sector. As a successful LIC agent for the past 30 years he accounted how best one can get remedy under Insurance Regulatory and Development Authority (IRDA).

In chapter eleven, S.S. Pankajam presented service problems in insurance sector citing her own case which she filed in Consumer Forum at Chennai. She points out that the R.N. Malhotra Committee made sweeping reforms in the insurance sector and brought in private sector to play their role. She laments that despite the provision of speedy disposal of cases; her case has been dragged for a long time and concludes by saying that there is need to stop such delaying/ miscarriage of justice.

In chapter twelve, R. Elangovan presented the general problems in the Public Distributive System in India. It is one of the services rendered by the state government agencies which are involved in many controversies and corruption. The existing deficiencies can be resolved the machineries of the national and state government machineries. The research scholar stressed the need for the consumer courts to come forward to pounced judgment on the lack of responsibilities and accountability when the public distribution fails to deliver its services.

In chapter thirteen, Mythili K. Rajendran vividly explained the role of government in protecting the interest of consumers. She concluded by saying that the future agenda for the government will be to encourage sustainable consumers and to develop and maintain mechanism which would enable exchange of information on national policies and measures in the field of consumer protection. The establishment of consumer clubs in schools and colleges would lead to increased awareness among the youth population of the nation.

In chapter fourteen, S. Ganga Bai presented that the consumer awareness programme in its expanded activity provides programme in schools. The programme to such awareness activity should be extended to colleges also as more and more people come to know about their rights and privileges. The consumer awareness programme must also be designed in such a way to impart its implications in every field of service providers instead of confining awareness programme in a general way. This definitely would help the people to know the deficiency in a particular Sector and to approach for relief. The effective programme may also be conducted in rural and semi-urban areas to benefit the rural and semi-urban people.

In the last chapter (Chapter 15) Dr. S. Ravishankar presented his views on banking services in India. He lauds the efforts of the Reserve Bank of India in establishing its own Ombudsman like bodies. Any aggrieved person can approach the banking Ombudsman to resolve their issues in relation to banking services. A modest attempt is also made to cite some important cases that were resolved by various redressal mechanisms to satisfy Customers/Consumers. However, there are many cases tried by the National Consumer Disputes Redressal Commission and made banking services more responsible and held accountable for various lapses.

NOTE

1. The Department is entrusted with the following works:

Internal Trade

Inter-State Trade: The Spirituous Preparations (Inter-State Trade and Commerce) Control Act, 1955 (39 of 1955).

Control of Future Trading: the Forward Contracts (Regulations) Act, 1952 (74 of 1952).

The Essential Commodities Act, 1955 (10 of 1955) (Supply Prices, and Distribution of Essential Commodities not dealt with specifically by any other Ministry/Department).

Prevention of Black-marketing and Maintenance of Supply of Essential Commodities Act, 1980 (7 of 1980). Persons subjected to detention there under.

Regulation of Packaged Commodities.

Training in Legal Metrology.

Emblems and Names (Prevention of Improper Use) Act, 1952 (12 of 1952).

Standards of Weights and Measures. The Standards of Weights and Measures Act, 1976 (60 of 1976).

The Bureau of Indian Standards Act, 1986 (63 of 1986).

Consumer Cooperatives.

All attached or subordinate offices or other organizations concerned with any of the subject specified in this list including Forward Markets Commission, Mumbai.

Monitoring of Prices and Availability of Essential Commodities.

The Consumer Protection Act, 1986 (68 of 1986).

Consumer Welfare Fund. (CWF).

REFERENCES

Ahmad, Farooq (1999). *Consumer Protection in India: Problems and Prospects,* New Delhi: Deep and Deep.

Arora, Renu (2005). *Consumer Grievances Redressal,* New Delhi: Manak.

Chaudhary, Ram Naresh Prasad (2005). *Consumer Protection Law: Provisions and Procedure,* New Delhi: Deep and Deep.

Consumer Protection Regulations.

Duraisingam, P. (2004). (Tamil) (Editor) *Nugarvor Theerppugal* published by FEDCOT, Chennai.

Himachalam, D. (1998). *Consumer Protection and the Law,* New Delhi: Deep and Deep.

Khandela, Man Chand (2001). *Consumer: Protection in India,* Jaipur: Shyam Prakashan.

Nugarvor Iyyengal Nooru (2004) (Tamil) (Editor) FEDCOT, Chennai.

Pye Lucian (1994). *Political Development.*

Sharma, Deepa (2002). *Consumer Grievance Redressal under the Consumer Protection Act,* New Delhi: New Century Publications.

Singh, Avatar (2002). *Law of Consumer Protection (Principles and Practice)* EBC-India.com, Lucknow.

Sivaprakasam, P., and Rajamohan, S. (2001). *Consumer Empowerment: Rights and Responsibilities,* New Delhi: Kanishka.
Srinivasan, K. (1999). New Era of Consumerism, *The Hindu*, October 31.
The Consumer Protection Act, (1986) *(68 of 1986)* 24th December.
The Consumer Protection Rules, (1987) (Amended up to 13.10.2006).
Venkatesha, H.R. (2005). *Consumer Protection in India: A Study of Karnataka State,* Jaipur: University Book House.

PART I

The Concept and Its Development

Chapter 1

New Challenges in Service Sector

HON'BLE JUSTICE K. SAMPATH

Consumer Protection

Introduction—Origin and History of Consumer Protection Law—Concept of Consumer Protection in Ancient India.

(a) In ancient India, professional and trade misconduct and negligence were very firmly dealt with.

(b) The king fixed the equitable price for marketable goods and products. In doing that he took into consideration various factors such as the distance from where they came, the place of there consumption, the freight, their value at origin, the incidental expenses incurred by the producer or the trader and the profit margin.[1] The sale or purchase had to be done only as per the kin's fixation. Transgression attracted severe punishment.[2] There were other social control measures. During the Mauryan Rule, Kautilya their legendary minister had introduced several such measure one of them being the creation of an independent department for weights and measures headed by a superintendent.

(c) He who tampered with scales, measures, royal mandate and standard coins, as also the person who used them, were liable to be fined the highest amercement.

(d) Where a trader, in his dealings with customers, deceived them by means of balances, measures of corm and measures of capacity that were not genuine, or by any other method was fined the first amercement.

(e) He who abstracted one-eight part by a false measure or balance, such a person shall be compelled to pay a fine of two hundred *panas*[3] or in proportion to the loss caused on that basis.

(f) Goldsmiths were to use the balance authorized by the State Goldsmith. For violation of the rule, punishment was a fine of 12 *panas*. A merchant who dealt in false gold and also one who sold unclean meat were maimed and also made to pay the highest amercement.

(g) The person adulterating (marketable) commodities was punished by a fine of the first amercement. A person who adulterated medicines, oil, salt, perfumes, grain, sugar and the like and kept them for sale was fined 16 *panas*.

(h) When earth, hide, gem, yarn, wood, fark or cloth was made to appear as, or misrepresented to be, of good quality when it was not of good quality, the fine was eight times the amount for which it was sold. A merchant who concealed the blemish of an article which he was selling, or mixed bad and good articles together or sold old articles (after repairing them) as new ones, was compelled to pay the purchaser double the value, and also a fine of an equal amount to the King.

(i) A person who dishonestly behaved with his customers or cheated them concerning price was fined with the first or the middle amercement. The merchants who subsisted by cheating in various ways during the course of selling different marketable commodities were open rogues (concealed rogues being burglars, robbers, etc.). They were caught by employing intelligent methods and punished commensurate with the gravity of the offence.

(j) Carriers were not spared. One who agreed to transport goods by carriage for consideration and agreed to deliver the same at a particular place within a specified time and failed to carry out the same was not entitled to charges.[4] If the consignment was damaged due to the carrier's fault he was answerable for the loss except when the damage was due to act of fate (God) or the sovereign.[5]

(k) The vicarious liability of masters and employers was in place. If the cart turned off the road owing to the driver's want of skill in driving, the owner was liable to be fined two hundred *panas* if damage was done. If the driver was skillful, but negligent, he alone was fined.[6] The master was liable to pay damages to third parties for the loss or injury caused to them by his servant.[7] Though they were termed as fines since they were payable to the affected parties they were only in the nature of damages.

(l) As regards builders if damage was caused due to improper construction of a building or carts etc., or by an unstable beam etc., the person responsible was liable to meet the cost of loss or medical treatment, etc.[8]

(m) Irregularity in the maintenance of accounts was punishable.[10]

(n) A physician who, though, not familiar with drugs and their effects or was ignorant of the nature of diseases, yet took money from the sick (for giving treatment), was punished like a thief.[10] All physicians who treated their patients wrongly were liable to pay fine. Growth of disease due to negligence or indifference of a physician was regarded as assault or violence. If the death of a patient under treatment was due to carelessness, the physician was punished with the middle level penalty (i.e. 500 *panas*).[11] The damages for medical negligence varied on the basis of the severity of injury or loss of life. In the case of wrong treatment of animals, the fine was the lowest.

During the Muslim Rule in India, particularly of Alauddin Khilji in whose reign prices of consumer goods were fixed at a very low rate within the approach of the poorest man, punishment was very severe for breach of the rates and weights.

Thus, it is not as if that 'consumer' concept is something new to us. It went from here to outside world and has come back to us.

General Background

(1) The right of safety;
(2) The right to be informed;
(3) The right to choose; and

(4) The right to be heard are regarded as the Magna Carta of Consumer's Rights.[12]

(a) In the late seventies, United Nations Economic and Social Council (UNESCO), on finding that consumer protection had an important bearing on economic and social development, requested the Secretary General of the United Nations to prepare a survey of national institutions and legislations in the area of consumer protection. In 1979, it made a further request for a comprehensive report containing proposals for measures on consumer protection for consideration by governments. The Council wanted a policy framework within which further efforts for consumer protection could be pursued. In 1981, therefore, it made yet another request to continue consultations with the aim of developing a set of general guidelines for consumer protection, particularly having in mind the needs of the developing countries.

(b) In 1983, the Secretary General of the United Nations submitted draft guidelines for consumer protection to the Economic and Social Council (UNESCO). Upon extensive discussions and negotiations among Governments on the scope and content thereof and taking into account the interests and needs of consumers in all countries, particularly those in developing countries, recognizing that consumers often face imbalances in economic terms, educational level and bargaining power, and bearing in mind that consumer should have the right of access to non-hazardous products, as well as importance of promoting just, equitable and sustainable economic and social development the General Assembly of the United Nations, adopted the guidelines for consumer protection which *inter alia* provide for the following objectives:

1. To assist countries in achieving or maintaining adequate protection for their population as consumers.
2. To facilitate production and distribution patterns responsive to the needs and desires of consumers.
3. To encourage high levels of ethical conduct for those

engaged in the production and distribution of goods and services to consumers.

4. To assist countries in curbing abusive business practices by all enterprises at the national and international levels which adversely affect consumers.
5. To facilitate the development of independent consumer protection.
6. To encourage the development of market conditions which provide consumers with greater choice at lower prices.[13]

"The United Nations passed a resolution in April 1985 indicated certain guidelines under which Governments could make law for better protection of the interests of the consumers. Such laws were more necessary in the developing countries to protect the consumers from hazards to their health and safety and to make available to them speedier and cheaper redress. Consumerism has been a movement in which the trader and the consumer find each other as adversaries. In the last two decades in many developed and developing countries powerful consumer organizations have come into existence and such organizations have been instrumental in dealing with the consumer protection laws and in the expansions of the horizon of such laws".[14]

"The Consumer Protection Act, 1986 was enacted as a result of widespread Consumer Protection movement. On the basis of the report of the Secretary General on Consumer Protection dated 27.05.1983, the United Nations Economic and Social Council recommended that the world Governments should develop, strengthen and implement a coherent consumer protection policy taking into consideration the guidelines set out therein. The governments were to further provide adequate infrastructure including the bodies as well as financial facilities to develop, implement and monitor consumer protection policies. The introduction of new products in the developing countries was to be assessed in relation to the local conditions having regard to the existing production, distribution and consumption patterns of the country or region concerned. With reference to the consumer movement and the international obligations for protection of the rights of the consumer, provision has been made in the said Act with the object of interpreting the relevant law in a rational manner and for achieving the objective set forth in the Act. A rational approach and not a technical approach is the mandate of law".[15]

The other important developments include:

(a) The 1981 World Health Organization (WHO) International Code of Marketing of breast milk substitute,
(b) The 1985 Food and Agriculture Organization (FAO) International Code of Conduct on the distribution and use of pesticides,
(c) The work in the area of food of the FAO/ WHO Codex Alimentarius Commission, and
(d) The United Nations General Assembly Resolution of December 17, 1982 on protection against products whose consumption and use have been banned, withdrawn, severely restricted or not approved by governments.

Legislation before Consumer Protection Act

All over the world, countries have passed legislation regulating and controlling unfair trade practice and protecting the interests of the consumer. India is not lagging behind. We have both pre-independence and post-independence laws enacted. Some of them are Indian Contract Act, 1872; Sale of Goods Act, 1930; Agricultural Produce (Grading and Marketing) Act, 1937; Drugs and Cosmetics Act, 1940; Drugs (Control) Act, 1950, Drugs and Magic Remedies (Objectionable Advertisements) Act, 1954; Prevention of Food Adulteration Act, 1954; Essential Commodities Act, 1955; Standards of Weights and Measures Act, 1956; Trade and Merchandise Marks Act, 1958; Essential Services Maintenance Act, 1968. The Monopolies and Restrictive Trade Practices Act, 1969; Prevention of Black Marketing and Maintenance of Supplies of Essential Commodities Act, 1980; Bureau of Indian Standards Act, 1986.

The above Acts have been passed to protect the interest of the consumer. The objects to be achieved are standardization, grading, packaging and branding, prevention of food adulteration, short weights and measures, hoarding, profiteering, etc. But then going to court under these Acts is a cumbersome, costly and long drawn affair and an ordinary consumer can ill afford the luxury. The benefit the small consumer has derived under these Acts is next to nothing. The Monopolies and Restrictive Trade Practices Act (MRTP Act) though promised the moon could not really help the small consumer. Though several recommendations were made by the Sachar Committee, to prohibit misleading advertisements, false representations, bargain sales, bait the tap selling, offering of gifts and prizes with intention of not providing them, conduction promotional contests, supplying goods that do not comply with safety standards and hoarding and distinction of goods, those could make little impact on what an average consumer wanted. Thus arrived the potentially consumer friendly legislation viz., The Consumer Protection Act in 1986, to promote and protect the rights of the consumer.

Salient Features of Consumer Protection Act

Who is Consumer?

Everybody is a consumer in some form or other. That means that every person is a victim in some way or the other of several unfair trade practices by unscrupulous business people. There is cheating in quantity, quality, price of goods or services. Once the maxim 'Caveat Emptor's'. Let the buyer beware which allowed the seller to disown his liability and enjoined the consumer to protect himself, was the standard slogan. But then in those days, perhaps, in village markets, products had less ostentatious exterior, no gloss and no sophistication and could be inspected before the purchase. One could perhaps count the teeth of the horse or the cow and fix the age before opting to buy or opt out. But things have changed over the years. People have little or no knowledge of the technologically manufactured products in today's mass production economy. Tall promises are made through exaggerated claims and advertisements baiting the trap for the unwary and they are invariably taken for a ride. The modern day's answer to 'caveat emptor' is the consumer law. Merchants and service providers cannot take the consumer for granted any more. Consumer is king and his satisfaction is paramount.

In the Statement of Objects and Reasons of the Act, it is provided as follows: It seeks *inter alia* to promote the rights of consumer such as—

(a) the rights to be protected against marketing of goods which are hazardous to life and property.

(b) the right to be informed about the quality, quantity, potency, purity, standard and price of goods to protect the consumer against unfair trade practices;
(c) the right to be assured, wherever possible, access to an array of goods at competitive prices;
(d) the right to be heard and to be assured that consumer interests will receive the consideration at appropriate forums;
(e) the right to seek redressal against unfair trade practices or unscrupulous exploitation of consumers;
(f) the right to consumer education; and
(g) These objects are sought to be promoted and protected by the Consumer Protection Council to be established at the Central and State levels.

The object of the legislation, as the preamble of the Act proclaims, is 'for better protection of the interests of consumers'. During the last few years preceding the enactment there was in the country a marked awareness among the consumers of goods that they were not getting their money's worth and were being exploited by both traders and manufactures of consumer goods. The need for consumer redressal fora was, therefore, increasingly felt. Understandably, therefore, legislation was introduced and enacted with considerable enthusiasm and fanfare as a path-breaking benevolent legislation intended to protect the consumer from exploitation by unscrupulous manufactures and traders of consumer goods. A three-tier fora comprising the District Forum, the State Commission and the National Commission came to be envisaged under the Act for redressal of grievances of consumers.[16]

One of the main objects of the Act is to provide speedy and simple redressal to consumer disputes and for the quasi-judicial machinery is sought to be set-up at the District, State and Central level. These quasi-judicial bodies are required to observe the principles of natural justice and have been empowered to give relief of a specific nature and to award, wherever appropriate, compensation to consumers. Penalties for non-compliance with the orders given by the quasi-judicial bodies have also been provided. The object and purpose of enacting the Act is to render simple, inexpensive and speedy remedy to the consumers with complaints against defective goods and deficient services. Prior to the Act, consumers were required to approach the Civil Court for securing justice for the wrong done to them and it is a known fact that decision in a suit takes years.[17]

According to Consumer Protection Act, 1986, a consumer is a person who buys any product or hires service for a price which has been paid in full or in part.

Health Care, Real Estate, Banking, Telephones, Electricity, Insurance or some of the areas of service where challenges are faced by the consumers.

Advertisements

Don't Always Trust Ads

Advertisements project false and exaggerated pictures and the people are unfortunately misled and buy those advertised products only to be disappointed. Just because an ad appears in a reputable magazine or newspaper, or on T.V. and radio stations, it is no guarantee that the product or service is legitimate. Only a few publishers and broadcasters are cautious about what ads they run.

But ads have their own positive and negative aspects:

- *On the positive side*—they give the consumer critical information so that he can take a decision whether to purchase a commodity or to avail a service.
- *On the negative side*—more often than not they do not give or project a correct picture and the consumer is misled.

There must be some law to regulate advertising particularly relating to health and health products—children and their food consumption patterns.

Banking

Of course banking is another service sector where things appear to have been made simpler and easier. But in reality they bring in their own problems. With a view to avoid your standing in the queue at the bank counters 'drop boxes' and 'standing instructions' concepts have been introduced. But then there are several instances where the cheques dropped in boxes do not reach the banks not having been collected in time with the result the customer is pulled up by the bank and penalized. So is the case with standing instructions. They are not followed and the constituents are put to untold misery.

Again day in day out you get calls and sasses offering credit card facilities. Your privacy is disturbed. The banks involved disown responsibility stating that the callers are not their employees. Consumer's right to privacy is abused by his being unduly disturbed by unsolicited cards, loans, credit enhancement etc. But then the banks who indulge in these are forbidden to do these things by the RBI. What do you do to prevent this? You tell your bank to include you in the list of constituents who do not wish to be troubled. (Do not call Registry) (Do not call numbers)

If you are in the habit of transferring money between accounts, make sure you get written confirmations so you can verify that the transactions went through correctly. Good, up-to-date record keeping will not only help you keep track of your money, but also will be useful, if your ever have a problem with your account.

Builder and Promoter

The complaints against builders and contractors are phenomenal in number. They violate the building rules with impunity, do not conform to the approved plans—use defective and fourth rate materials do not complete the construction within the time stipulated in the agreement between the parties—of course the buyer also is to blame—he does not keep the payment schedule. As a consumer, he should fulfil his side of the bargain. If defects are noticed get a licensed engineer to assess the same and go to the Consumer Court after calling upon the builder to rectify the defects.

Honey soaked words turn sour once you are hooked and fall a prey....

False advertisements as if some reputed bank would offer attractive loans for purchasing/building flats. It would turn out that there is no approval, there are deviations, banks do not check whether the plans are sanctioned and the corporation/municipal demolition squad is at the door.

The builder does not keep the schedule, uses third rate materials, are long cracks develop and your headache starts, never to end. Perhaps you were also at fault. You did not have a check list—nor did you stick to the payments schedule. As a consumer you should fulfill your side of the bargain. If defects are noticed, get a licensed engineer to assess the same and go to the consumer court after calling upon the builder to rectify the defects.

Carriage of Goods by Road, Rail, Air and Sea

The liability is that of an insurer. The general principle is that they should prove absence of negligence on their part.

Courier Services

Courier Services are yet another area where consumers face problems. They have unilateral liability disclaimer clauses stating that in cases of any loss or damage to the consignment or for any other reason, their liability shall not exceed Rs. 100. But then Consumer Fora have entertained complaints and given relief holding they are unilateral liability disclaimers and unless the complainants have been put on notice of the terms and conditions of the acceptance of consignment and have been parities to the same. Much more needs to be done to make courier services more responsible.

Terms and conditions on consignment not binding consignor. However, liability limiting clause in small print and explained to complainant—not binding. The clause will not deter commission from awarding reasonable compensation. However, limitation of liability has to be brought to the notice of the complainant. Consignee is beneficiary of service entitled to maintain complaint. Failure to deliver letter. Courier Company can be held liable for deficiency in service.

Educational Service

Student taking examination of University is not a consumer. However, imparting of education for consideration is service. Misrepresentation by Educational Institutions will attract the Consumer Protection Act. Students admitted in violation of rules and regulations can maintain complaints under the Consumer Protection Act. Personal information regarding date of viva is not given is not deficiency in service. Educational Institutions can be held guilty of unfair trade practice. Failure to rectify error in certificates would attract the Consumer Protection Act. Deficiency by School authorities in treating student who was injured would attract the Consumer Protection Act. It is, however, open to the school to demonstrate that the course of treatment adopted was proper. Disputes relating to service conditions cannot be agitated in Consumer Forums.

Electricity

Electricity Department unable to rectify defects for a long period is liable to pay compensation. Short circuit on account of negligence on the part of the Electricity Board—complainant can maintain action.

(a) Defective meter-complaint directed to be charged on the basis of the readings for the past six months.
(b) Refusal to give connection as department contended that complaint had committed theft of electricity-complaint untenable.
(c) Surge in electric current resulting in loss. Electricity Board directed to compensate.
(d) Delay in giving electricity connection constitutes deficiency in service. Failure to supply electricity to a agricultural fields will attract the Consumer Protection Act.
(e) Tennant who avails electricity connection of landlord is consumer. If there is violation of terms of supply by consumer, he cannot maintain complaint.
(f) Death caused by electrocution will attract the Consumer Protection Act.
(g) Inflated bills can be directed to be revised.

Health Care

The children see the advertisements on TV and press the parents to buy what they have seen. The parents find it difficult not to concede their demands. And what happens. The children become ill. The next thing you do is to go the hospital.

What does the Doctor do?

Digressing here for a minute—Have you heard of Kalki?

He fell ill. He went to the doctor. Why? the doctor has to survive.

The doctor gave a prescription. Kalki took it to the pharmacist and bought the medicines. Why? The pharmacist has to make a living.

As he entered his house, he put the medicines in the drain. Why? He has to live? This is only by the way.

The parents go to the doctor. The doctor has a laboratory attached to his clinic or hospital. It is his own but run in somebody else's name. The lab has to carry on. Hundreds of tests have to be carried out—necessary and unnecessary—the doctor has an X-ray unit that has to be run on profitable lines. More specialist doctors have more sophisticated facilities—depending on what the traffic can bear these have to be undergone.

Doctors are very often charged with unethical practices. Selling of medicine samples to the patients, stocking and selling of medicines without licence, open promotion of products of certain companies for a consideration, suggesting tests where unnecessary and above all charging an exorbitant fee for consultation. Indian Medical Council (Professional Conduct, Etiquette and Ethics) Regulations, 2002 do try to sort out the deficiencies but then it is such an arduous task for the Medical Council of India and the State Medical Councils.

Some of the deficiencies that doctors could be accused of are:

(a) The doctor does not give immediate treatment in urgent cases;
(b) The doctor does not take precaution as per the medical jurisprudence of giving the test does of medicines which are likely to be fatal in some cases or may cause allergy;
(c) In some cases the patient gets into serious problems due to wrong administration of anesthetic drugs;
(d) The post-operative treatment is not given properly;
(e) The surgical wound is caused at a different place than required;
(f) After operation, septicemia or gangrene takes place;
(g) Improper prescription of drugs. In case of fever, without knowing the cause of fever, combination of tables and injections for malaria, typhoid, etc., are freely used;
(h) Medical instruments are left in the body;
(i) Mal-practice by the doctors, such as uncalled for pathological reports or investigations prescribed;
(j) Apparent error in giving higher doses of anti-biotics or steroids resulting in adverse effect;
(k) Not giving complete case papers to the patient at the time of discharge from the hospital; and

(!) In big hospitals, particularly, government hospitals, proper arrangements are not made patients are required to wait in long queues for hours together.

In case of gross deficiency in service by an advocate, has person may loss the case, he may lose some money or property. But, in the case of negligence by doctors, the person is affected adversely. He may lose his life. The deficiency in medical service is of utmost concern in the present day society.

As already noted, we are having the Indian Medical Council Act, 1956 under which several States should have Medical Councils and at National level there should be a Medical Council of India. These have to be made functional and effective so that persons instead of approaching the Consumer Fora or the courts could get reliefs from the experts in the field. If the experts arrive at the conclusion that there was negligence or deficiency in service either by the hospitals or by the doctors, Civil Court or the Consumer Fora can grant appropriate compensation. This would also reduce the work load of the Consumer Fora.

When a patient comes to a private clinic, he goes by the reputation of the clinic and with the hope that proper care will be taken by the hospitals authorities. Most often, when a person goes to a hospital the patient does not know which doctor will treat him. The patient relies on the hospital and clinic to engage the best doctors for him. The Supreme Court in *Savita Garg vs. Director, National Heart Institute* {(2004) 8 Section 56}, has observed that it is the responsibility of the clinics that they must provide for the best of services when they charge for the services rendered to them. Very significantly, it has also been observed that in case it is found that the service rendered by the clinic or hospital, as the case may be, is not up to the mark and involves negligence as a result of which the patients suffer, they are bound to reimburse them.

The next question is when we can say the service is not up to the mark? Deficiency under Section 2(g) of the Consumer Protection Act, 1986 is defined as follows:

> It means *"any fault, imperfection, shortcoming or inadequacy in the quality, nature and manner of performance which is required to be maintained by or under any law for the time being in force or has been undertaken to be*

performed by a person in pursuance of a contract or otherwise in relation to any service." The word 'deficiency' is of the broadest connotation. It means any fault, imperfection or shortcoming or inadequacy in the quality, nature and manner of performance of the service."

Deficiency of service is not mere medical negligence. It is something more. The treatment of patients and their family members by the hospital authorities and the staff would also constitute deficiency in service. Whether it is a question of conducting of tests or whether it is a question of organizing blood or medicine, the family members of the patient are made to run from pillar to post. In *Spring Meadaws Hospital and others vs. Harjot Ahluwal* {(1998) 4 Section 39} it has been noticed by the Supreme Court that in the garb of doing service of humanity doctors have undertaken commercial activities, and have been mercilessly extracting money from helpers patients and their family members and yet they do not provide the necessary services. Several hospitals have become cold, uncaring and unsympathetic institution in which not only the patients but also the family members are treated with callous indifference and sullen arrogance in the secure knowledge that the persons are helpless and have nowhere else to go. The hospital staff must be trained in proper administration of the hospitals and the proper treatment not only of the patients but also the family of the patients. Hospital Authorities should develop procedures and train staff to—

(a) inform the patient as accurately as possible the nature and extent of his illness;
(b) inform the patient of available treatment to enable the patient to determine the best possible course of treatment;
(c) inform the patient of any negative effects of the treatment;
(d) maintain strict privacy with regard to the medical history and condition of the patient lest it may be misused or taken advantage of except where is not revealed would cause injury to a third party;
(e) the medical practitioner ought not to administer treatment not expressly consented to by the patient; and
(f) pre-operative procedures and training in this regard to be given to hospitals staff.

No person can get entry into a hospital without a huge deposit being paid. If a person is covered with medical insurance, he should be allowed to walk-into the hospital without having to make any deposit. It is a human disaster if an ailment takes place over the weekend and a person is not in a position to muster up enough cash for making the deposit. Insurance Companies should tie up with the hospitals so that the insured person can indicate the hospital of his choice where the policy can be registered and at the time of admission, the fact that the person is insured would be enough so as not to require him to make any cash deposit. There is a practice followed by most hospitals in having varying and different rates for the same treatment depending on the type or class of room occupied. It is understandable why the fees payable to the doctor, the rate charged for tests and the charges for various equipments should vary depending on the nature and category of the room. All the charges for the investigation process including tests and scans vary. If a patient is admitted to a lower category room and is later transferred to a higher category all the charges are also revised retrospectively.

Our doctors have skills which match international standards and the king of equipment now available in our hospitals and is at the disposal of our doctors is increasingly better. But, the doctors should not be mere doctors. They should be healers. A person cannot be a healer unless he understands the needs and shortcoming of the people who come to him.

Hospitals, it is reported inflate bills with the collusion of insurance people. Keep a close watch. When bills are raised by hospitals double check them. If they are artificially inflated you will have problem in availing the remaining value of the future.

To illustrate—say you are insured for Rs. 1 lakh. Your actual hospitalization charges come to say Rs. 25,000 But it is inflated to Rs. 40,000 Instead of Rs. 75,000 left you will have only Rs. 60,000 to bank on.

Insurance

Insurance is yet another area where the consumer faces serious problems.

What is Insurance?—It is a means by proposer/consumer transfer the risk of a potential loss to the insurance people for a fee and when the loss occurs, the company pays up. A very simple and ideal principle. But in practice the consumer confronts a lot of problems before he sees the colour of the coin.

In my view, both are to blame, particularly in the matter of mediclaim policies. More often than not the proposer does not give full information, conceals or suppresses material facts or signs on dotted lines and the proposals form is filled up with false or wrong details by the agent of the insurance company giving a handle later on to the insurance company to plead suppression entitling them to repudiate liability. It pays to answers questions honestly on applications for health insurance. If you file a claim for treatment for a condition you did not previously reveal, the insurance company, after checking out your medical history—may deny your claim based on the false information given on your application. The company is also free to cancel your policy.

At the time of taking the policy itself, a mechanism has to be evolved to eliminate suppression. Well there is this problem, if that is done, there will be less buyers of policy and many insurance companies may have to close down.

The insurance people have to project a more human face. They should stop using the means as a private business opportunity. Insurance is an essential social welfare measure.

School

Failure of school to address safely issues will attract the provisions of the Act. In a case a child studying in school fell into an open septic tank and drowned. National Commission held that keeping a tank open near toilets where tiny tots study was an act of sheer negligence on the part of the school authorities. It also held parents of the child had hired the services of the school and therefore are consumers and the school was responsible for the safety of the children studying in it during school hours and therefore the school was guilty of negligence and deficiency in service.

Theft

Cars and two-wheelers get stolen from parking lots of cinema houses, hotels and other public places. The question is who is liable? Whether the owners of those places?

The service providers almost always rely on disclaimers displayed or printed parking at owners' risk. No liability will attach to the owner of the place in case of the theft, damage or loss. Consumer Courts have held that they would be liable except when the owners of the vehicles had left them unlocked and unsecured.

Disclaimers by themselves cannot absolve the owners of premises of their liability. Consumer is now considerably armed. But then he should exercise his right without accepting the disclaimers as impenetrable walls.

Warranties

Do not accept a sales person's oral promise that the company will take care of anything that goes wrong. Proving such a statement is almost impossible. Get any such promises in writing and have it singed by a manager or someone else in authority. Of course, you may find that no one is willing to do this. If that's the case, you then know that the promise is worth exactly as much as the paper it's not written on.

General

Under Section 14 of the Act, if after the proceedings conducted under the Act, the Forum concerned is satisfied that the goods complained against suffer from any of the defects specified in the complaint or that any of the allegations contained in the complaint about the services are proved, it may direct anyone or more of the following things:

(a) to remove the defect,
(b) to replace the goods,
(c) to return the price,
(d) to pay compensation for loss or injury suffered by the customer,
(e) to remove the defects or deficiencies in the services in question,
(f) to discontinue the unfair trade practice or the restrictive trade practice or not repeat it,
(g) not to offer the hazardous goods for sale,
(h) to withdraw the hazardous goods from being offered for sale, and
(i) to provide for adequate costs to parties.

If the Opposite party fails or omits to comply with the order made against him, under Section 27 of the Act, he shall be punishable with imprisonment for a term which shall not be less than one month but which may extend to three years, or with fine which shall not be less than Rs. 2,000 but which may extend to Rs. 10,000 or with both. Depending upon the circumstances, the Forum concerned can impose lesser term or lesser fine. Frivolous, malicious or vexatious complaints can be dismissed with costs of upto Rs. 10,000.

Hiring of service is essential for alleging deficiency in service in complaint.

There can be complaint regarding non-payment of deposits as also for non-payment of employee provident fund benefits.

Purchase of seeds for agricultural purposes is not purchase for commercial purpose and would attract the provisions of Consumer Protection Act.

Deficiency in conduct of lottery cannot attract the provisions.

Defect in goods would attract Consumer Protection Act. In a particular case complaints had bought chicks from the first opposite party. The chicks were reported to have been vaccinated for the disease "Merek" by the second Opposite party. The chicks did not yield the desired production of eggs. Later the chicks died. It was alleged that either the chicks were not administered the vaccine for Merek disease or the vaccine supplied was defective. The post-mortem report indicated that the chicks died of Merek disease. The State Commission dismissed the complaint. On appeal National Commission held that the purchase by the appellants was for self-employment within the ambit of the Act, but on merits it was held that since the sample of the vaccine was not tested and no investigation had been done, no liability could be fastened to the respondents. The appeal was dismissed. [*G. Hanumath Reddy vs. Singh Poultry Ltd.* (2000) 1 CPJ 26 = 2000 (1) CPR 15 (NC)].

Illustrations

- Injuries suffered on account of defective pressure cooker would entitle award of compensation.
- Registration department does not render service as contemplated under the Act.
- Cultivator entering into agreement with sugar factory is not a consumer.

- Complaint against Panchayat is not maintainable.
- Complaint by shareholder of co-operative society against society is maintainable.
- With regard to grant of loan, if there is *bonafide* exercise of discretion deficiency in service will not be made out.
- Repair of watches—hirer of services entitled to maintain complaint even if he is not owner of goods.
- Payment of tax would not amount to payment of consideration.
- Commercial purpose—tests to determine.

The question that came up before the Supreme Court for decision was whether the complaint had been using the machine "Brickman" for clay preparation, brick moulding, brick drying and brick burning after purchasing the same from the appellant for earning his livelihood by way of self-employment or whether the purchase could be said to be for commercial purpose. The Supreme Court held that the mere fact that the respondent is earning a livelihood in commercial business does not mean that it was not for self-employment. Supreme Court held that the burden of proving the question lies on the respondent and also the question was matter of evidence. Whether the respondent was using the machine by himself and the members of his family for preparation and manufactures and sale or whether he employed workmen and if so how many were matters of evidence and the burden is on the respondent to prove them. Supreme Court held that the tribunals were not right concluding that the respondent is using the machine only for self-employment and that therefore is not a commercial purpose.

Constructing the scope of the term "exclusively for the purpose of earning his livelihood by means of self-employment" the Supreme Court held as follows:

"The explanation excludes from the ambit of commercial purpose in sub-clause (i) of Section 2(1)(d), any goods purchased by consumer and used by him exclusively for the purpose of earning his livelihood by means of self-employment. Such purchase of goods is not commercial purpose. The word 'self-employment' is not a commercial purpose. The word 'self-employment' is not defined. Therefore, it is a matter of evidence. Unless there is evidence and on consideration thereof it is concluded that the machine it was used only for self-employment on regular basis the employee or employment. Manufacture and sale of bricks in a commercial way may also be to earn livelihood, without sense of commercial purpose by employing on regular basis the employee or workmen for trade in the manufacture of bricks in commercial way may also be to earn livelihood, but merely earning livelihood in commercial way also be to earn livelihood, but merely earning commercial business does not mean that is not for commercial purpose. Self-employment connotes altogether a different manufacture by employing himself in working out or producing the goods for earning his livelihood. "He includes the members of his family". Whether the respondent is using the machine exclusively by himself and the members of his family for preparation, manufacture and sale of bricks or whether he employed any workmen and if so how many is matters of evidence. The burden is on the respondent to prove them".

Shortfall in quantity-purchase would be for commercial purpose.

Purchase of truck for self-employment—complainant is a consumer.

If there is deficiency in service during warranty period, complainant would be consumer under the Act.

Purchase of poultry concentrate by small farmers is not purchase for commercial purpose. However, purchase of eggs for resale is purchase for commercial purpose.

Issue of community certificate by RDO is a duty which does not involve any hiring of service for consideration and is not covered by the Consumer Protection Act. [Revenue Divisional Officer, Madurai vs. Sakkarai Pandi (1995) 2CPC 666=1995 (3) CPR 351 NC)]

Electrocution of cow-claim against electricity board is not maintainable in Consumer Court. Assurance to purchase sugarcane-failure to do so-there is no consumer dispute involved. Mere agreement to purchase goods will not attract the Act.

Wrong entries in Encumbrance Certificate can make the Registrar the provision of the Act. If the plants are affected on account of inferior seed quality, the provisions of Consumer Protection Act would be attracted. Jurisdiction of consumer for not excluded by Seeds Act.

Defects in vehicle, tractor, etc, will attract the Consumer Protection Act and the dealer and manufacturer can be held liable. Defective fabric, defective water meter, contaminated soft drinks, will all attract the Consumer Protection Act.

However, beneficiary under rural debt relief scheme is not a consumer and he cannot invoke the Consumer Protection Act. Member of a co-operative society is a consumer.

Consumer Association cannot seek relief independent of the relief sought by consumer. Consignor is entitled to maintain complaint regarding deficiency against Transport Company.

Equally, bus service can be held for deficiency in service in charging fare twice.

Consumer Rights

1. Right to satisfaction of basic needs.
2. Right to safety and security.
3. Right to information.
4. Right to choice.
5. Right to representation.
6. Right to healthy environment.
7. Right to consumer education.
8. Right to redressal.

Consumer Responsibilities

1. Critical awareness and vigilance.
2. Being involved and active.
3. To practice sustainable consumption—Social concern.
4. Concern for the environment to be responsible to the environment.
5. Working together—to be organized and fight for justice.

Common Problems Faced by Consumers

Consumer Rights Violations

1. Under-weighing,
2. Adulteration,
3. Improper billing,
4. Poor quality goods/spoilt or damaged goods,
5. Poor maintenance,
6. Hidden clauses in contract—cheating on contract terms,

7. Price over and above MRP,
8. Unwanted goods thrust on consumers,
9. Misleading advertisements aimed at the children in particular,
10. Expiry date over medicines being foisted on consumers,
11. Bogus companies,
12. Overcharging interest especially in credit purchase, and
13. Dangerous, hazardous or unsafe goods being sold.

Lack of education is one big hurdle in our endeavour to achieve consumer friendly atmosphere.

Indeed the Act provides the consumer a very cheap remedy through information and speedy protection. Parties need not engage lawyers. They can present their case themselves or through representatives or through recognized consumer associations. Again under Section 4(d) of the Legal Services Authorities Act, 1987; the National Services Legal Authority, i.e., the central authority has the function to take necessary steps by way of social justice litigation with regard to consumer protection... There is thus direct involvement of the Central Government in the country in public and social interest apart from its *locus standi* under Section 2(1)(b)(iii) of the Consumer Protection Act.

NOTES

1. Manu VIII 401-402 and Yajnavalkya II 253—Justice M. Rama Jois—*Legal and Constitutional History of India*; I Edition.
2. Yajnavalkya II 249, 250.
3. '*pana*' means a silver coin.
4. Manu VIII 156.
5. *Narada* p. 1451.9; *Dharmakosa* p. 850.
6. Manu VIII 293-294.
7. Justice M. Rama Jois.
8. Justice Rama Jois.
9. Kautilya pp. 64-65.
10. Brihaspati 360-8.
11. Manu IX 284.
12. In March 1962, U.S. President John F. Kennedy in his message to Congress outlined the above as a Consumer's Bill of Rights.
13. State of Karnataka *vs.* Vishwabharathi House Building Co-op. Society (Sinha, J.), (2003) 113 Comp Cas 536 = AIR 2003 SC 1043 = (2003) 2 SCC 412, Para 6, 418.

14. Spring Meadows Hospital *vs.* Harjot Ahluwalia, (1998) 4 SCC 39 = AIR 1998 SC 1801 = (1998) 92 Comp Cas 797.
15. (Para 4) India Photographic Co. Ltd. *vs.* H.D. Shourie, {(1999s) 6 SCC 428 = AIR 1999 SC 2453)}
16. Common Cause, A Registered Society *vs.* Union of India (2002) 6 SCC 730=1993 (1) CPJ 1).
17. 2:07:35 PM 12/10/2006 (J.J. Merchant (Dr.) *vs.* Shrinath Chaturvedi {(2002) 6 SCC 635 = AIR 2002 SC 2931)} (Para 7).

Chapter 2

Ancient Views on Consumer Rights and Remedies

R. THIAGARAJAN

The Consumer Protection Act, to protect the interest of Consumers was enacted in 1986, but the trace or sources of this Act could be found in the Ancient laws that date back to approximately 2000 years. In those days Smrti or the law books was considered as a 'member' of the Kings Court. Narada, a writer of Smrti says, "Attending to the dictates of law books and adhering to the dictates of the Chief Justice, let a King try Causes in due order. It is plain therefore that the Smrtis were the recognized authorities' both in the King's Court and in the popular tribunals." When two Smrtis disagreed, sage Yajnavalkya opines, "that Smrti prevailed which followed equity as guided by the practices of the old." Thus, our ancient law givers have laid down rules of procedure and pleading in great detail.

Eighteen titles of law containing detailed rules are mentioned by Smrti writers. They are:

(a) Recovery of debt,
(b) Deposits,
(c) Sale without Ownership,
(d) Concerns among Partners,
(e) Resumption of gifts,
(f) Non-payments of wages,
(g) Non-performance of agreements,
(h) Rescission of sale and purchase,
(i) Disputes between the master and his servants,

(j) Disputes regarding boundaries,
(k) Assault,
(l) Defamation,
(m) Theft,
(n) Robbery and violence,
(o) Adultery,
(p) Duties of man and wife,
(q) Partition and inheritance, and
(r) Gambling and betting.

A bare perusal of these titles of law sufficient show the Composite and Comprehensive character of ancient Hindu Law: it was partly in usage, partly rules and regulations made by the rulers and partly decisions arrived at as a result of experience.

Brhaspati says that there are four kinds of laws that are to be administered by the king in the decision of a case. The decision in a doubtful case is by four means, DHARMA, VYAVAHARA, CARITRA, and RAJASASANA. Dharma refers to moral law or rules of justice, equity and good conscience. Vyavahara refers to civil law as laid down in Smrtis. Caritra refers to custom and Rajasasana refers to king's edicts or ordinances. With these preludes, we may identify the roots of contemporary legislation on consumer rights and remedies. At the outset let us examine a few salient points of valid and invalid transactions.

The sages declare that the transaction of a woman have no validity, especially the gift, hypothecation, or sale of a house or validity. Such transactions are valid when they are sanctioned by the husband or, on failure of the husband, by the son or on failure of the husband and the son by the king. In the same way, the transactions of a slave are declared invalid, unless they have been sanctioned by his master. If a son has transacted any business without authorization from his father it is also invalid. A boy becomes a major after the age of sixteen and independent only in case his parents are dead. While they are alive he can never acquire independence even though he reached mature age. If a boy or one who possesses no independence even though he reached mature age. If a boy or one who possesses no independence transacts anything it is declared invalid. If a person is independent but lost control of actions, transacts anything that is invalid for want of real independence. Those are declared to have lost control of actions are actuated by love or anger or tormented (by illness) or oppressed by fear or misfortune biased by friendship or hatred.

Lending Money

Lending money is approved as in the case of Bankers today. 2, 3, 4 or 5 per cent is the legitimate rate of interest, but the virtuous practice is 2 per cent interest is fourfold—periodical; stipulated: kayika (diminishing the principle) and compound interest. When a creditor receives payment he must gives a receipt to the debtor. If he does not give a receipt, although he has been asked for it, he shall lose the remainder of the sum due to him.

If the repayment amount by the debtor is not receipted the sum shall yield interest to the debtor (hence for the) as it had done to the creditor previously (witness is insisted in such cases). Recovery of money from sureties was also in vogue. A creditor may recover his money lent through legal proceedings, by fraud, by the customary mode and filthy and by force. The customary mode is variously explained as denoting fasting or taking family asset, etc. It is almost similar to sitting in '*Dharna*'. There are details about documentations. A document committed in writing is superior to witnesses.

These are the day, the deposits of money or articles are cheated by the depositories and freely escape causing the depositors suffers a lot. The ancient view is that 'If the depositing fails to restore the deposit to the depositor, he shall be compelled to restore by forcible means after his guilt has been proved by or deals etc. Depositor must be restored precisely in the same condition as they were in at the time of their delivery. The wicked man, who fails to return the deposit on being asked to do so by the depositor, shall be punished by the king. If the deposit has been lost or destroyed, he shall make good its value. If he derives profit from a deposit by using it without the consent of the depositor, he shall be punished likewise and shall restore the profit together with interest to the depositor. He, who fails to restore a deposit and he who demands what he never deposited shall both be punished like thieves and shall be made to pay sum equal to the value of deposit. When properly kept as a deposit or the property of a stranger lost (by him) and found (by another man) or stolen articles, are sold in secret, it has to be considered as a sale effected by another than the rightful owner. When a chattel, which had been sold by another person than the owner, has been recovered by the owner, he may keep it. No blame attaches to a sale effected in public, but a clandestine sale is viewed in the same light as theft according to law.

If a man buys from a slave who has not been authorized to sell by his master, or from rouge, or in secret or at a very low price or at an improper time, he is as guilty as the seller. The purchaser must not make a secret of the way of his purchase. Otherwise he is equally guilty with the vendor and shall suffer the punishment of a thief. The vendor shall restore his property to the rightful owner and shall pay to the buys the price for which it was sold to him; besides that he shall pay a fine to the king.

Hired commodities shall be restored by the hirer when the fixed period has expired. The hirer must make good whatever may have been spoiled or destroyed except in the case of inevitable accident.

Non-Delivery of a Sold Product

Movable and immovable properties are termed merchandise regarding purchase and sale. The rule regarding the gifts and receipts of merchandise is six fold. i.e. what is sold by tale (guarantees), by weight, by measure, according to work, according to it beauty and according to its splendour.

If a man sells property for a certain price and does not hand it over to the purchaser, he shall have to pay its produce. If it is immovable and the profits arising out of it is movable property.

If there has been a fade in the market value of the article in question, the purchaser shall receive the difference of amount. This is applicable to the inhabitant of the same place. This is not applicable to a foreigner as he can make up the difference in foreign currency.

If the articles sold should have been injured or destroyed by fire, or carried off. The loss shall be charged to the seller, because he did not deliver it after it had been sold by him.

When a man shows one thing which is faultless and delivers another thing with blemishes. He shall be compelled to pay twice its value to the purchaser and an equal amount as fine.

When a man sells something to one person and afterwards delivers it to another person, he shall be compelled to pay twice its value to the purchaser and a fine to the king.

When a purchaser does not accept an article purchased by him, which is delivered to him, the vendor commits no sin by selling it to a different person. When the price has not been tendered there is no offence to be imputed to the vendor except in the case of a special agreement.

It is for the sake of gain that merchants are with habit of buying and selling merchandise of every sort. That gain is in proportion to the price either great or the reverse.

Therefore, shall merchants fix a just price for their merchandise, according to his locality and season and let them refrain from dishonest dealings. Thus by adhering these principles trade becomes an honest profession.

Revision of Purchase

When a purchaser after having purchased an article for a price, thinks he has made a foolish bargain, he may return it to the vendor on the same day, in an undamaged condition.

When the purchaser returns it on the second day, he shall lose a thirtieth part of the price. He shall lose twice as much on the third day. After that time the purchaser is bound to keep it.

The intending purchaser shall first examine an articles (before purchase) in order to find out the good and bad qualities. That which has been approved by the purchaser after through examination cannot be returned to the vendor.

Cattle may be examined for three days; animals of burden for five days; and in the case of precious stones, pearls and coral the period of examination may extend over seven days.

Bipeds shall be examined with in half a month; all sort of grain with in ten days; iron and clothes with in a single day.

A worn gown, which is in a ragged condition and soiled with dirt, cannot be returned. Wearing apparels losses the eight part of its value on being washed for the first time. The fourth part after second wash, the third part for the third time and one-half for the fourth time.

Sage Yajnavalkya stipulated that gold, when heated for conversion, would not lose any weight (Compare this with modern prevalent practice of the loss factor inherent in the conversion of the precious yellow metal into jewellery). However, it is conceded that silver, the precious white metal was bound to lose two per cent of its weight when it is subject to the process of heating and conversion. Tin and lead would lose about 8 per cent. Losses beyond these stipulated margins were severely frowned upon.

For the manufacture of embroidered, *Zari* bordered, gold-laced cloths (*dhotis*, upper garments, *saries*, other such approved), etc. proportionate losses allowed, consistent with the manufacturing technology keeping in mind the interest of the trader and consumer. Supervision and control of weights and measures was yet another area through over seen by the experts. Generally, the profit margins were pegged at 10 per cent only.

REFERENCES

Bahler, G., *"The Laws of Manu"* (New Delhi: AVS Books Distributors).

Chandrasekar, N. (1958). *"Hindu Law and Usage"* (Madras: Higginbotham).

Jolly, Julius (1889). "Narada Brhaspati" Part I in Maxmuller. F, (ed.) *"The Sacred Books of the East"*, Vol. XXXIII (Oxford: The Clarendon Press).

Jolly, Julius (1928). *"Hindu Law and Custom"* (Calcutta: Greater India Society).

Chapter 3

Consumer Rights Override Outlived Protection Laws

B.P. CHANDRAMOHAN

India has many protection laws to safeguard the interests of the consumers. Seldom these laws are used for protecting the rights of consumers rather than been used to harass the trading community. Hence by ensuring consumer rights, he may be able to safeguard him from exploitation as and when he requires it. The compliance of rights is easy and cheap when compared to the protection laws.

So far traders have been treated badly by the executives in the name of consumer's protection. But traders are also an important component of Indian economy where trading of goods and services play a significant role. It stood around 13.4 per cent of the GDP and employed approximately 36 million people. During the decade of 1990-91 to 1999-2000, the growth rate of trade was 6.9 per cent. Trade facilitates exchange of commodities and services. It creates markets comprising various goods and services. The goods and services are embodiment of division of labour in a society. Various infrastructural facilities like transportation and communication helped expand the scope of trade in goods and services. Local trade brings division of labour on a small scale while national and global trade ensures division of labour on a large scale. With the expansion of trade, there is a need to increase the facilities like processing, storage, package and transportation. Credit and insurance are added characteristics of trading activity. More trade facilities the state favourably disposed towards collection of higher taxes. Hence measures causing retardation in the growth of trade will necessarily affect the growth of the economy. The traditional protection laws and orders caused serious damage in the growth of trading activities.

The trading community in India faces diversity of controls exercised by multiple authorities at different levels restricts interregional movement of goods, lack of uniformity and taxes. These features break the large Indian market into a large number of smaller regional markets. This chapter examines various difficulties in the compliance of traditional control, regulations and licenses in terms of time and resources, possibilities of corruption and malpractices. Too many controls and regulations will instigate inefficiency of trading practices and ultimately reduce the consumers' welfare. Consumer welfare depends upon competition among sellers in terms of price and quality. Any violation of the responsibilities of traders against the consumers by false promises, price and quality is liable to punishment. Hence, consumer's rights will play a better measure when compared to the traditional laws, controls and regulations.

The independent India enacted various laws in the name of consumer protection. At present there are more than 400 laws that govern the trade. Some of the laws outlived their utility and appear arbitrary. The following are some of the laws cited as examples of outlived and arbitrary.

Essential Commodities Act, 1955

Prior to the third amendment of the Indian Constitution in 1955, regulating trade was the responsibility of the State Government. After the third amendment, regulation of production, prices and distribution of essential commodities came under the control of the union government. The Essential Commodities Act, 1995 (ECA, 1995) enshrines the provisions of regulating licenses and permits, increasing cultivation of foodgrains, controlling prices, prohibiting the withholding of essential commodities, regulating transactions, collecting information, etc.

Generally the ECA, 1995 classified commodities into items of mass consumption (food stuffs), commodities of agricultural origin (fodder, vegetables, etc.), intermediate products (insecticides, fungicides, etc.) and industrial products (iron and steel). The ambit of items included in each head becomes pervasive and the number of items is far more than can be gauged. For instance, under the category of iron and steel include all items manufactured by using iron and steel. This is the same with regard to the category of foodgrains also. The ECA, 1955 is an umbrella legislation under which state governments impose all kinds of restrictions on storage, transport and processing of agricultural produces. These restrictions were justified on the grounds that they would be necessary to control hoarding and other types of speculative activity. They rarely worked in times of genuine scarcity. The realistic assessment of the performance of ECA is that they were misused by the lower strata of the administration and it became an instrument of harassment and corruption.

During the regimes of New Economic Policy the need to relax various controls on agricultural products was discussed in the Chief Ministers Conference in May 2001. Though they have decided to continue ECA, 1955 as the umbrella legislation, the need for dismantling controls and restrictions was recognized. As a result of it in 2002, dealers are allowed to freely buy, stock, sell and transport foodgrains at any quantity.

Weights and Measures Act, 1976

The Weights and Measures Act, 1976 (WMA, 1976), deals with the establishment of standard weights and measures. The Standard Weights and Measures Enforcement Act, 1985 deals with the regulation and enforcement of weights and measures of industrial production, trade and commerce. The complexity is that the establishment of standard and weights is the responsibility of central government; the enforcement is placed under the concurrent list, while the implementation is vested with the state governments. Therefore, the establishment is uniform throughout the country but the declaration requirements desired by the enforcement machinery differ from state to state.

Orders Related to ECA, 1955

There are various orders pronounced under the ambit of ECA, 1955. Each order in one way or other paved the way for corruption and non-compliance. The following are some of the orders and their limitations.

State Levy Control Orders

Various state levy control orders have been introduced under the ambit of ECA. Based on the order the private rice mills have to deliver between 7 and 75 per cent of their processed output for the Food Corporation of India (FCI) and to the respective state government for the Public Distribution System (PDS) and buffer stocks. For these deliveries the mills receive the Minimum Support Price (MSP) for paddy plus the average milling cost. After meeting these commitments, the private mills can sell their remaining output in the open market. The compulsory levy of rice is prejudicial to the rice millers because the individual hullers and sellers do not have to make any contribution towards levy.

Sugar Control Order, 1966

The ECA outlines the guidelines for price determination of the levy sugar supplied by the producer. The levy sugar price fixed by the government is on the basis of the minimum sugarcane price, manufacturing cost of sugar, tax payable thereon and a reasonable return on capital employed. The sugar control order, 1966 empowers the government to regulate production of sugar, restrict the sale of sugar in the open market, and regulate the movement of sugar quality control, entry search, sampling and seizure of sugar. Though the regulation is aimed at controlling the price of sugar and ensuring availability it gives tremendous pressure to the producer of sugar.

Milk and Milk Products Order (MMPO)

The MMPO came to existence in June 1992 under ECA. This Act seeks to ensure the supply of liquid milk, an essential commodity, by regulating the processing and its distribution. The salient features of MMPO are the establishment of an advisory board, registration of big processing units, preferential treatment to cooperatives, hygiene etc. The MMPO empowers the authorities to enter, inspect and seize in case of non-compliance and power to cancel or suspend their licenses. The MMPO is criticized for the reason that it restricts private sector investment.

In addition to these orders, there are a number of orders viz., Meat food products order (1973), Fruit products order (1977), Pulses and edible oils order (1977), Cotton control order (2000), Jute and Jute textiles control order (2000), etc. require a thorough revision in order to protect the growth of their industry without hurting the interests of the consumers.

Agriculture Produce and Marketing Acts

The National Commission on Agriculture (1976) recommended regulated markets for agricultural produces. Various systems of sale are in vogue even in regulated markets. The basic objective of market regulations is to regulate the trade practices, increase market efficiency through reduction in market charges, elimination of superfluous intermediaries and protecting the interests of producer sellers. The functioning of the regulated market reveals that these objectives were not adequately achieved.

Prevention for Food Adulteration Act, 1955

It is the principal instrument to ensure the supply of clean and wholesome good of human consumption to the public. The Act by itself is not a complicated piece of legislation; however, the accompanying rules are Byzantine in nature. There are also a number of procedural problems in the implementation of the law. The law requires the food inspectors to pay for the samples that they take in the presence of atleast two witnesses. In practice no one will like to act as a witness. Even if they come forward, they used to give fictitious name and addresses which cannot be traced at the time of the issue of summons.

Need of Consumer Rights

The explanations given above are some of the practical difficulties while implementing the Acts, orders, regulations and controls. Though there are hundreds of such legislations, the consumers are seldom protected from adulteration, exploitation or cheat but the trading activity has been seriously affected due to unnecessary interventions, harassment and corruptions of the officials in the bottom rungs of administration. This is not only common to the trading activities of India alone but common to many developing and developed countries. The need for protecting consumers by empowering them was the feasible and economical option available before the United Nations. Hence, in order to protect the rights of consumers, the United Nations adopted the UN guidelines for consumer protection in April 1985. The guidelines call upon the governments to maintain a strong consumer policy for the enhanced protection of the consumers. In consonance with the UN guidelines, the Government of India enacted Consumer Protection Act in 1986.

Consumer Protection Act, 1986

Some of the issues, especially consumers' economic interest have been covered under the MRTP Act, 1969 and it has been modified from time-to-time. In fact, the Consumer Protection Act, 1986 provides' a better approach for protecting the interest of the consumers. The public transaction cost of this approach is minimal while consumers are empowered to protect their rights through various means.

In order to provide speedy, simple, specific and inexpensive redress to consumer disputes through summary trails, three-tier quasi-judicial machinery was introduced under this Act. They include one national commission, 35 state commissions and 570 district forums. The forums are required to dispose cases, as far as possible within 90 to 150 days. Apart from these forums, consumers can also approach the civil courts and other legal forums. The Consumer Protection Act has been amended twice in 1991 and in 1993. It now provides a central consumer protection council as the apex body for safeguarding consumers interests. The council is supposed to meet once in a year to review the progress in regard to consumer awareness and consumer protection.

In the era of Globalization and Multinational Corporations it becomes imperative to protect consumers from different kinds of onslaughts. There are different methods used to safeguard the interests of the consumers.

Maximum Retail Price (MRP)

Manufacturers have to mention the maximum retail price on the packaging of goods. MRP was made mandatory to protect consumers' interest against overcharging by the retailer. This has lost its relevance since goods are sold at half of the MRP price. So the consumers' interest remains unprotected. However, it provides some protection to the consumers. Subsequent to the revision of excise laws, excise duty collections are linked with MRP in specified cases which acts counter to high MRP marking.

Consumers as Investors

In India small investors have suffered a great deal in recent years. Fly-by-night finance companies have lured the gullible public, especially the retired employees and petty business people by promises of high returns. The loopholes of the regulatory provisions have led to the investors being cheated. Thus the poor enforcement laws embolden white collar criminals. Recently, the government took various steps to close the gap between the regulations and the possibility of the escape of criminals.

Housing

Housing is an area where consumers face a number of problems from construction firms. While building houses consumers face the problems of delays in the completion of construction, cost escalation and sub-standard material quality. Housing constitutes the single most life time expenditure item of an average customer who undertakes the building work by availing loans from banks. Rating systems and self regulatory organizations need to be created and strengthened for protecting the consumers.

Public Utilities

Many public utilities like the railways, the postal system and telecommunications continue to operate under outdated anti-consumer rules and regulations. The right to information about the cause of accidents, loss, etc. is not readily provided and the rules framed are not transparent. These may be reviewed in the light of best practices prevalent in other countries.

It is fair if the affected party or person makes complaint against the supply of a purchased good or a service rather than adopting umbrella legislation. In India many regulations are outlived their utility and they cause severe damage to the trading activities. If we want to remove these barriers, the country needs to introduce reforms in laws. Legal reforms may be initiated for a simple transparent and business friendly system. There should also be a comprehensive self-regulatory legislation relating to consumers rights and consumer sovereignty.

Chapter 4

Consumerism in the Service Sector

A. SETHURAMASUBBIAH

The year 1986 has a special importance and significance in the legal history of our country. The three legal instruments, viz. Environmental Protection Act, Child Labour Prohibition and Regulation Act and The Consumer Protection Act were enacted by our Parliament. The commonalities of these three legal instruments are the pro-activeness and the protectiveness on the one hand and that they need awareness among masses to make these laws more meaningful and purposeful. To quote the famous legal adage "Justice not only to be done; but it should be seen to be done" would be right as these three laws are beneficial to the common man and to the society only when they are honoured in both letter and spirit. However, the unfortunate state of affair is that these three legal instruments have not achieved the desired effect neither on the violators nor among the victims.

For as long as there has been exchange of *goods and services* between buyers and sellers, the ultimate success of all economic activity has depended upon producing *goods and services* that the buyer considers suitable. When one thinks of the consumerism, consumer right, etc., the *goods* only comes to mind and in most situations the *services* are left untouched in an ambiguity whether such *services* are covered by the Act or not.

The consumerism in the West is entirely different from that of ours. The reasons are obvious—education, enlightenment and awareness among the people. However, in the Indian context, even after two decades, we are still a long way to go in the matter of consumerism, consumer protection and enforcement of the same. Though there are cases filed in the consumer forum, most of them are related to '*goods*' only and the '*services*' are given little importance as there is no clarity on the matters related to '*services*'.

The Consumer Protection Act, 1986, is applicable to '*all goods and services*'. The Act defines, *inter alia,* a consumer as "any person who hires or avails of *any services* for a consideration which has been paid or promised, or partly paid or partly promised, or under any system of deferred payment and includes any beneficiary of such services other than the person who hires ...when such services are availed of with the approval of the first person mentioned." Thus the consumer has every right to be protected in terms of services availed by him.

The following cases are given from the records of to throw more light on the 'services' category to create awareness among the masses.

1. ICRPC run NGO assisted the Mumbai Police and traced the absconding Chairman, Mr. Rajesh Jaiswal of Srushti Group of Companies and arrested him at Lucknow. This person was absconding since 5 years after committing financial fraud. The properties of the Srushti Group are attached through the court. The investors will get their money from the sale proceeds of these properties.
2. Full course fee refunded to Mr. Parminder (Tel. No. 0130-2241642/2242651) from APTECH against consumer complaint for their low grade educational services. The case was filed at Sonipat (Haryana) but was withdrawn due to out of court settlement through our notice.
3. Telephone user gets refund for excess money charged by MTNL Thane, and receives compensation for mental agony and harassment.
4. Train passenger gets full refund of the railway fare from the Central Railway due to late running of train.
5. Student of Vijay Mukhi classes, Anisha Mehta (Tel. No. 28076777) of Mumbai got full refund of the fees through the action of ICRPC when she was not satisfied by the standard of teaching by Mr. Vijay Mukhi and when Mr. Vijay Mukhi refused to refund her fees.
6. Sanjit Chatterjee (*e-mail*: sanjit/mro_-_tata_steel@mro.tatasteel.com) receives refund of his money against complaint

regarding poorly functional stock direct account of Stock Holding Corporation of India Ltd.

7. Anita Bommanaveni of USA (*e-mail*: abommana@ford.com) complained to us regarding non-refund of medical insurance claim of her mother Mrs. Kalavathi Puli (Tel. No. 0870-2431867) residing at Warangal, from United India Insurance Company Ltd., Chennai. The Manager Mr. Subir Bhattacharya vide letter dated 25.3.2003 agreed to settle the claim of the consumer immediately after the company received our notice. The complainant received Rs. 2.28 Lakh on 16.6.2003 as full and final settlement.
8. Mr. A. G. Godbole (Tel: 079-7461922) of Ahmedabad, complained to us about non-transfer of his post office fixed deposit from Bhilai (MP) to Ahmedabad. Through the intervention of ICRPC, the deposits were immediately transferred to the concerned branch on 12.3.2003.
9. Mr. Hitesh P. Kakadia (Tel: 0253-2519108), student of Mahatma Gandhi Vidyamandir's Dental College and Hospital, Nashik, complained to the consumer forum (ICRPC) that he was being forced by the college principal to pay a fee of Rs. 2,31,000 while the prescribed fee was Rs. 86,000. Our notice to the principal had immediate effect and the correct fee only was collected from the complainant.
10. Standard Chartered Bank at Mumbai deducted the EMI amount from the savings bank account of the consumer, Mr. Prabir Chetia, even after he submitted necessary papers for foreclosure of his loan account. Consumer Forum's notice to the bank resulted in refund of Rs. 3,000 to the consumer on 12.8.2003.
11. Mrs. Varsha Pandey of Sagar (MP) did not receive her revalidated dividend from Unit Trust of India since February 1998. Repeated reminders did not fetch any results. When the consumer did not receive the cheque even after five years, she complained to ICRPC. The consumer received the amount within 30 days after we issued notice to UTI in August 2003.
12. A notice dated 6.8.2004 was sent to the ICICI Bank by ICRPC, seeking refund of excess EMI deducted by the bank

from the consumer Mr. Arun Pratap Chattopadhyay (Tel. No.: 080-51172852). The bank credited the amount of Rs. 21,474.00 and sent confirmation letter to the consumer on 17.8.2004.

13. Mrs. Meena Sharma (Tel. No. 27703352) of Nerul, Navi Mumbai, complained to ICRPC about deficient services by her dentist Dr. R.K. Tuli. On receipt of the forum's notice on 1.11.2003, the doctor accepted his deficient services, and agreed to redo the full treatment up to her satisfaction.
14. Ms. Madhu Midha Roy of New Delhi did not receive her B.Ed. degree certificate from Annamalai University for last 10 years, even after continuous calls to the Registrar. ICRPC issued a notice and the consumer received her degree on 8.12.2003, within 10 days of our notice.
15. Mr. Dhananjay Pole of Hyderabad (Tel. No. 040-23225090) started receiving bills from Reliance Infocom even though he does not own their mobile phone. When his efforts to contact Reliance Infocom to settle his grievance became futile, he contacted ICRPC. The consumer later received a written confirmation from Suyash Saraogi, Vice-President, and Reliance Infocom that the said telephone number has been disconnected as precautionary measure and the grievance redressed.
16. State Express Transport Corporation Tamil Nadu Ltd. *(A Government of T.N. Undertaking)* sent their Senior Officer to a consumer's house to apologize for causing inconvenience to him during the bus journey. This happened as soon as ICRPC sent a notice to the SETC seeking compensation for the inconveniences caused to the consumer.
17. Mr. S. Saravana Ayyakutti (Tel: 0462-2552058) travelled from Tirunelveli to Chennai by State Express Transport Corporation Tamil Nadu Ltd. *(A Government of T.N. Undertaking)* on 25.11.2004. He asked the conductor to provide him the front seat as it was vacant, and because he had injury in his right leg, he wanted to straighten his leg as per doctor's advice. The conductor was rude and did not allow him to sit on the vacant front seat. The grieved consumer complained to ICRPC who issued a notice to the

Chairman of SETC-TN. The Chairman immediately sent their Branch Manager to the consumer's house to apologize for causing inconvenience to him during the bus journey. The officer also promised that there would be no inconvenience to him in the future.

18. Mr. Alok Mohanty complained to ICRPC that he won Play win lotto and he did not receive the amount. ICRPC issued a notice and the money was immediately transferred to the consumer's account.
19. Mrs. Jalaja Menon of Navi Mumbai did not receive the maturity amount by Cable Corporation of India Ltd. even after surrendering the original FD certificates. ICRPC warned Cable Corporation of severe action. The FD maturity amount was released and was paid on 5.3.2004.
20. The consumer had requested Thane Head Post Office on 5.6.2004 for ECS facility on post office fixed deposit (MIS). When nothing happened for 3 months, ICRPC sent a notice to Postmaster General on 15-9-04 by fax. ECS account was opened the same day with the post office senior staff visiting the consumer's home asking for apology.
21. Mr. Hasim Shroff (Tel: 26317528) of Mumbai was to receive Rs. 43,000 from his relative based in Dubai through the services of UAE Exchange on 26.3.2005. But the UAE exchange delayed the delivery of money and finally on 20.4.2005 they told the consumer that he has already received this amount on 16.4.2005, which he never did. The consumer approached Mr. Mohammed Afzal of ICRPC and he issued a notice to the UAE Exchange. The company immediately paid the full amount to the consumer.
22. The consumer, Mr. Srikanth (Tel: 9242486662) booked for Bombay to Chennai by Air Deccan. His flight was delayed for more than four hours. ICRPC sent a notice dated 8.7.2005 to Air Deccan. Full amount was refunded to the consumer in July 2005.
23. Mrs. Manonmani (Tel. No. 022-25402476) held jointly (either or survivor) Fixed Deposit—MIS Account No. 5537 at Head Post Office, Thane. Her husband expired in 1999. When she approached the Post Master for refund of her

maturity amount, he refused to pay the money. Some clerks were expecting a bribe, and were harassing her. When Mrs. Manonmani complained to ICRPC, a notice was issued to the Post Master General. Full amount of Rs. 4,50,000 was paid to Mrs. Manonmani on 22.9.2005.

24. Mr. Bharat Kelbaikar of Mumbai (Tel. No. 9820520992) had paid full amount by cheque on 24.10.2005 for booking a room at Regal Hotel, Mahabaleshwar through their Mumbai agents Pradeep and Company of Matunga, Mumbai. The consumer cancelled his booking on 26.10.2005, but the agent did not refund his amount for the reason that according to the terms and condition printed overleaf the receipt that "deposits will be forfeited if reservation is cancelled". When ICRPC wrote to them that their terms and conditions on the receipt also stated that "We do not accept cheques", then why they broke their own rules by accepting the consumer's cheque for booking the room. The consumer was given a fresh booking for other date, and was allowed stay in the Hotel in the month of November 2005.

25. Mr. Ayyappan Shankaran of Mumbai (Tel. No. 56002601) had subscribed to the "Good Health Policy" for one year i.e. expiring on 28.2.2005, but Citibank continued to charge him for the same as was reflected in the bill of March 2005, even when he had not renewed the policy. The bank also charged the consumer for "Credit Shield Policy" for which he had never applied. The Citibank even went to the extent of sending "*goondas*" (some third class cheap recovery agency) to harass the consumer for payment for something which he had not even subscribed for. The consumer had brought this to your notice of higher authorities of the bank but they slept over this matter and continued to harass the consumer. Finally the consumer complained to ICRPC. ICRPC lashed on the Chairman of Citibank about his cheap "*dadagiri*" and threatened him with severe action if he did not stop his goondaism. Immediate action was taken and the consumer was informed by e-mail dated 6.12.2005 that the bank has reversed the excess charges.

Thus the Consumer Protection Act, 1986 is really a mighty weapon in the hands of the consumer. But the harsh reality is that it is not exposed to the masses properly. The so called sensitive ambassadors, the students should be educated properly and the message if consumerism shall be diffused into the community with commitment.

Chapter 5

Unfair Trade Practices

C.M.K. THAMPI

Historical Background of Consumer Movement in India

The protection of people against economic exploitation had existed for several hundred years. During middle ages, the dishonest traders had their hands cutoff, a trader selling shoddy goods would be dragged around the town with his ware tied around his neck. In Kautilya's *Arthashasthra*, there are references to the concept against exploitation by trade and industry. We find reference to unfair trade practice, food adulteration and punishments to be meted out to the erring traders in the laws of Manu. But in those days of barter system the consumer and the producer/trader knew each other personally and there was little scope for the producer or trader to cheat the consumer.

Need for Consumer Protection

The consumers have to be protected from the aggressive sales promotion efforts of the trading community. So there is a need of well organized, non-violent, vigilant wide spread consumer organization to promote and protect the consumer welfare and prevent the malpractices of unscrupulous retailers, quick profit seeking peddlers and unethical manufacturers. The Consumer is totally neglected element in the market though he is responsible for the creation of economic activity.

Thus consumerism is not a new phenomenon. In the early 1900's and again during the Great Depression in 1930s, there was a 'Consumer Movement'. Efforts were made to protect the consumer from harmful products and from false and misleading advertising. The Sovereignty of consumer is not a truth but only a myth. It prevails only in theory rather than in practice. The consequent need to give protection to the consumers from nefarious activities, exploiters has sprouted the entire world over.

Pro-Consumer Legislations Enacted in other Countries

In United Kingdom for Instance Trade Description Act, 1968; prohibits the use of misleading representation of price reductions etc. The Sherman Act and the Clayton Act of the USA, the Federal Act of Switzerland, the Act against Restraint of Competition of Spain, the Act concerting prohibition of Private Monopoly and Maintenance of Fair Trade in Japan, the Trade Practices Act of Australia, the combines Investigation Act of Canada, etc., are a few to mention. As per the United Nations Guidelines all the countries were directed to enact separate Consumer Protection Legislation.

Pro-Consumer Legislations Enacted in India

Numerous Laws were enacted by the Government to safeguard the interest of the consumers. To name a few –The Essential Commodities Act, 1955; The Agriculture Product (Grading and Marking) Act, 1937; Monopolies and Restrictive Trade Practices (MRTP) Act, 1969; Patents Act, 1976; The Weight and Measurement Act, 1976; The Environment Protection Act, 1986; The Consumer Protection Act, 1986, etc.

The MRTP Act, 1969 and Unfair Trade Practice

The passing of the MRTP Act, 1969 could be said to be the beginning of Governments concern for consumer interest. Sachar Committee highlighted the need for introduction of suitable provisions to curb unfair trade practices like misleading advertisements and false representations, bargain sales, bait and switch selling, offering of gifts and prizes without any intention of providing the same, conducting promotional contests, etc. Accordingly the MRTP Act was amended in 1984 to incorporate Section 36 A to 36 E relating to "Unfair Trade

Practice" with effect from 1st August 1984. The MRTP Amendment Act, 1991 had widened the scope of Unfair Trade Practice.

Scope of MRTP Act, 1969

The MRTP Act, 1969 was a giant step in recognition of rights of the consumers in India. The aim of the Act was not to make the consumer, sovereign of the market but to prevent the concentration of economic power in the hands of few private individuals. However, the consumers came to acquire many invaluable rights against the monopolistic, restrictive and unfair trade practices indulged in by the unscrupulous traders and trading houses. The Act also helped the emergence of consumers a class by themselves who subsequently became a powerful force to reckon with India. By no stretch of imagination it can be said that the Act of 1986 has diluted the spirit of MRTP Act but it had strengthened its base and application.

Enactment of the Consumer Protection Act, 1986 and Unfair Trade Practice

When the Consumer Protection Act (CPA) was enacted in 1986, it did not contain the definition of 'Unfair Trade Practice'. This concept was frequently interpreted in MRTP cases because Monopolies and Restrictive Trade Practices Act, 1969 contained the definition of "Unfair Trade Practice".

Unfair Trade Practice Under MRTP and CP Act

The Consumer Protection (Amendment) Act 1993 incorporated an exhaustive definition of "Unfair Trade Practice" in Section 2(1)(r) CPA with a view to making CPA a self-contained Code. The said definition is virtual reproduction of the definition of "Unfair Trade Practice" as in Section 36A of MRTP Act. Until such incorporation by 1993 Amendment Act, whenever, the concept of Unfair Trade Practice was to be interpreted vis-a-vis CPA, the definition for unfair trade practice under Section 36A of MRTP Act 1969 was referred along with case laws decided hereunder. It was therefore considered necessary to have statutory regulations insisting that, while advertising, the sellers must speak the truth, according to Section 36A to 36E in part B inserted in chapter 5 of MRTP Act.

Object of Definition

'Honesty and truth' in manufacturer-customer relationship.

These observations of Supreme Court were followed by Monopolies Commission in *Achal Kumar Galhotra vs. Byford Motors Ltd.*[1]

The advertisement which was restrained by the commission was that the dealer was offering Premier Padmini at Rs. 28,000/- less than Maruti. There was no indication of the market price of Maruti. The offer of a free stereo was also false because the cost was recovered by inflating the registration charges the scheme of replacing the car of a lucky purchaser with a new car every year by drawing lottery was held to be untenable by virtue of the provisions in Section 36-A (1)(3) of MRTP 1969 and Section 2 (1)(r)(3) of CP Act 1986.

Unfair Trade Practice as defined in Section 2 (1)(r) of CP Act 1986.[2]

An Unfair Trade Practice means a trade practice, which, for the purpose of promoting any sale, use or supply of any goods or services, adopts unfair method, or unfair or deceptive practice.

Unfair Practices may be Categorized as Under—

1. False Representation: [Section 2(1)(r)(1)]

The practice of making any oral or written statement or representation which:

(a) falsely suggests that the goods are of particular standard, quality, quantity, grade, composition, style or model;
(b) falsely suggests that the services are of particular standard, quantity or grade;
(c) falsely suggests any re-built, second-hand, renovated, reconditioned or old goods as new goods;
(d) represents that the goods or services have sponsorship, approval, performance, characteristics, accessories, uses or benefits which they do not have;
(e) represents that the seller or the supplier has a sponsorship or approval or affiliation which he does not have;
(f) makes a false or misleading representation concerning the need for, or the usefulness of, any goods or services; and

(g) gives any warranty or guarantee of the performance, efficacy or length of the life of the goods, that is not based on an adequate or proper test.

Makes to the public a representation in the form that purports to be—

(a) A warranty or guarantee of the goods or services,
(b) A promise to replace, maintain or repair the goods until it has achieved a specified result,
(c) If such representation is materially misleading or there is no reasonable prospect that such warranty, guarantee or promise will be fulfilled, and
(d) Gives false or misleading facts disparaging the goods, services or trade of another person.

2. False Offer of Bargain Price—[Section 2 (1)(r)(2)]

Where an advertisement is published in a newspaper or otherwise, whereby goods or services are offered at a bargain price when in fact there is no intention that the same may be offered at that price, for a reasonable period or reasonable quantity, it shall amount to an unfair trade practice.

The 'Bargain Price' for this purpose means

The price stated in the advertisement in such manner as suggests that it is lesser than the ordinary price, or the price which any person coming across the advertisement would believe to be better than the price at which such goods are ordinarily sold.

3. Schemes offering Free Gifts Offer and Prize Schemes [Section 2(1)(r)(3)]

The unfair trade practices under this category are—

(a) Offering any gifts, prizes or other items along with the goods when the real intention is different;

(b) Creating impression that something is being offered free along with the goods, when in fact the price is wholly or partly covered by the price of the article sold;

(c) Offering some prizes to the buyers by the conduct of any contest, lottery or game of chance or skill, with real intention to promote sales or business; and

(d) Withholding from participants any scheme offering gifts, prizes or other items free of charge, on its closure the information about final results of the scheme.[3]

4. Non-compliance of Prescribed Standards [Section 2(1)(r)(4)]

Any sale or supply of goods, for use by consumers, knowing or having reason to believe that the goods do not comply with the standards prescribed by some competent authority, in relation to their performance, composition, contents, design, construction, finishing or packing, as are necessary to prevent or reduce the risk of injury to the person using such goods, shall amount to an unfair trade practice.

5. Hoarding, Destruction or Refusal [Section 2(1)(r)(5)]

Any practice that permits the hoarding or destruction of goods, or refusal to sell the goods or provide any services, with an intention to raise the cost of those or other similar goods or services, shall be an unfair trade practice.

Spurious goods, Deceptive Practices: [Section 2(1)(r)(6)][4]

It is an unfair trade practice to manufacture spurious goods or to offer such goods for sale. Adoption of deceptive practices in the provision of services has also been recognized as Unfair Trade Price (UTP).

Doctrine of Caveat Emptor replaced by Caveat Venditor

In the early law, the doctrine of "Caveat Emptor"—"let the buyer beware" was the philosophy of law of sales. Today it has been replaced by "Caveat Venditor "—"Let the seller beware". As a result of this change of legal philosophy, business is heavily regulated on behalf of the consuming public. 'The Consumer must get what he is told he is getting'. Where, by any method whatsoever, a belief is created in the minds of consumers as to some quality or utility of goods/services and they actually fall short of these standards, this will be unfair to the consumers.

Such methods listed in the section above are regarded as an Unfair Trade Practice. This is so because the primary theme of the provisions is to protect the consumer from the business community.

Five ingredients of Unfair Trade Practice as laid down by Supreme Court in *Lakhanpal National Ltd. vs. MRTP Commission.*[5]

(a) There must be a trade practice within the meaning of Section 2 (u) of the MRTP Act.
(b) The trade practice must be employed for the purpose of promoting sale, use or supply of any goods or the provisions of any services.
(c) The trade practice should full within the ambit of one or more of the categories enumerated in Clauses 1 to 5 of Section 36 A of MRTP Act
(d) The trade practice should cause loss or injury to the consumers of goods or services.
(e). The trade practice under clause (1) should involve making a statement whether orally or in writing or by visible representation.

Analysis of Decided Case Law in Different Service Sectors with Respect to Unfair Trade Practice

Defective Jewellery—Unfair Trade Practice—Proved

The statement of objects and reasons of the Consumer Protection Act of 1986 underlines the right of the consumer to be informed of the quality, potency, purity, standard and price of goods to protect the consumer against unfair trade practices.

In Hanuma vs. Meena Jewellers,[6]

Where the respondent did not mention the purity of ornaments in the bill and by marking 22/18 on the ear-top, made the quality ambiguous. The consumer's right to be correctly informed of the purity standard was thus impaired. If "tunkum" is used in making ornament and thus the cartage is reduced, the purity or standard of the gold should have been clearly mentioned on the ornament and in the bill. Making any statement whether orally or in writing or by visible representation which falsely represents that the goods are of a particular quality or standard, or materially misleads the public concerning the price, amounts to unfair trade practice.

In such circumstances, failure to mention purity or standard of gold in the bill and collecting price as if it is 22 carat gold is nothing but an unfair trade practice. By marking the purity of the gold in the bill, it amounts to imperfection or shortcoming in purity or standard. Therefore, it is a defect.

Medical Services—False Advertisement was amounting to Unfair Trade Practices

The complainant had Ulcer on leg. He saw eye catching advertisement by MQM Hospital that it will be completely cured by importing vaccine. He was treated for about 15 months but his Ulcer did not subside. His condition aggravated and he had to be admitted to another Hospital. Held, that this ailment was incurable and patient was not informed about it. This material fact was suppressed and the treatment was prolonged which amounts to unfair trade practice.[7]

Education Services —Admission to course without getting application from University

Since the students were admitted to the course without getting affiliation from University and no proper steps were taken by the college to enable them to appear for examinations, then it is deficiency in service and unfair trade practice on part of Principal of College and State Government and giving stipend to students is no reason, not to treat them as consumers.[8]

Delivery of Car — Time Essence of Contract — Unfair Trade Practice Proved

The complainant a handicapped person had booked an automatic transmission car with the Opposite party. The Opposite party had issued a letter dated 4.03.1991 for deposit of balance price for delivery of car within two weeks but the car was delivered on 1.11.1999. By that time excise duty had been increased. On complaint it was held that as time was the essence of the contract, the circumstances for non-delivery had not been proved by the Opposite party. Therefore, it amounted to deficiency in service and also unfair trade practice.[9]

Dry fish booked by complainant but fish manure supplied—Unfair Trade Practice Proved

Where goods delivered were entirely different from the goods booked, unfair trade practices were proved and Opposite Party was liable to refund the cost.[10]

"Scratch and Win"—Card—Unfair Trade Practices Proved

In Bonn Nutrients Pvt Ltd. vs. Jagpal Singh Dara.[11]

Petitioner launched a Sale Promotion Scheme of the bread manufactured by it under the brand name "Bonn". Under the scheme in each purchase of bread a coupon with slogan "scratch and win" impliedly gave guarantee that every person purchasing bread will win one of the prizes mentioned in the advertisement. Respondent purchased bread with coupon having word only " Please try again"

Held: Complainant held guilty of Unfair Trade Practice.

Dead Bea found in Soft Drink "Fanta"—Deficiency in Service Proved.

In C. C. Chellappan vs. Chennai Bottling Co Ltd.[12]

Manufacturing and selling soft drinks to the public should be free from components injurious to health. The complainant purchased 2 bottles of a soft drink with brand name "Fanta" for consumption, on opening the bottle he found a dead big bee in it. Selling such a product to Common Public will not only be injurious to public health, but also would amount to unfair trade practice, besides being deficiency in service.

Held: State commission confirmed the order of the District Forum with direction not to offer for sale such hazardous goods in future.

Defective Car not Rectified—Deficiency in Service

In Tata Engineering and Locomotive Co. Ltd. vs. Sri Chandrashekar & Others.[13]

The Complainant purchased Tata Indica Diesel Car from opposite party. Defects such as leakage of oil from the engine and other general defects as pointed out were not rectified, even after free service.

Held: There is an inherent manufacturing defect. Vehicle is not up to the satisfaction as per the advertisement and Manufacturer has failed to rectify the same Opposite party directed to replace the engine and pay damage and cost. Appeal filed by Opposite party was disunited.

Prize Scheme—Scratch Card—Deficiency in Service and Unfair Trade Practices Proved

Mohammed Ayub Khan Soudagar vs. Amjad Attar and Others.[14]

Here the complainant purchased Biscuits worth about Rs. 580 but could not get scratch cards after handing over empty wrappers to participate in draw to be held on 7th Feb 2001.

The Product Manufacturer M/s. Britannia Industries Limited offered to issue prize money of 1 crore. The complainant was not provided with the scratch card which deprived him from participating in KBC (draw) suffered mentally.

Held: Deficiency of service by delaying the delivery of scratch cards by the retailer not issues scratch cards in time amounts to gross unfair trade practice. The commission directed the opposite parties to pay Rs. 1 lakh as compensation along with interest a cost.

Purchase of Computer—Unfair Trade Practice and Deficiency in Service Proved

In Dr. (Mrs.) Neeraj Kalra vs. Harpreet Singh.[15]

The applicant a doctor by profession needed computer for professional/personal use. Computer delivered by respondent started malfunctioning within 3 months of purchase when RAM of the machine got damaged. Missing accessories were also not given in time. The respondent turned deaf ear to the repeated requests made. There was sheer deficiency in service.

Held: Applicants allegation of Opposite party indulging in Unfair Trade Practice stood proved. Entitled to get compensation.

Builder—Deficiency in Service

In J. Mallika vs. A.V. Balaguruswamy.[16]

Complainant entered into an agreement with the opposite party for construction of a residential apartment and for conveyance of 33per cent of undivided share. Price was also paid. The opposite party failed to make any arrangement for construction or conveyance of undivided share. Price paid was not returned.

Held: Directed to return the advance amount along with interest. Compensation for mental agony and cost was also awarded.

Misleading Advertisement in "Fair & Lovely" Cream amounted to UTP

The Managing Director Hindustan Lever Limited vs. S.T. Rajan.[17]

The complainant purchased "Fair & Lovely" cream for fair complexion and used the same for 6 weeks as advertised. No such effect and improvement in the skin was noticed as represented through the advertisement released. Complaintant claiming compensation for unfair trade practice under Section 2(1)(r) of CP Act was allowed in the lower forum. The statement made in the advertisement amounts to guarantee and representation is about quality and standard of product. Appeal preferred by the manufacturer was dismissed and confirmed the order of the lower forum. They are further directed under Section 14(i) (hc) of CP Act 1986 to issue at their cost corrective advertisements to neutralize the effect of misleading advertisement made so far.

Protection of Consumers against Unfair Methods or Deceptive Practices

In order to protect and prevent such practices the producer and all the element of distribution channel has to give due regard to the consumer rights. The producer has an inescapable responsibility to ensure efficiency in production and quality of output. He should resist the temptation to charge exorbitant prices in a seller's market. He should avoid hoarding black marketing, etc. We can see that for an effective protection of consumer rights the producers, consumers, Government and consumer organization play a vital role. The Advertising Media and Marketing Management too have a very important role to play in this respect. They should avoid misleading and false representations.

The Government has to come to the rescue of the helpless consumer to prevent him from being misled or cheated or exploited. Statutory action to protect the interests of the consumers has become quit common.

Relief Measures provided under the Consumer Protection Act

If the forum is convinced that goods were really defective or that complaint about services is proved true the forum shall issue an order directing the opposite party to do any thing as stated in Section 14 of the CP Act, 1984.

MRTP Act, 1969 repealed and replaced by Competition Act 2002

MRTP Act, 1969 has become obsolete in certain respects in the light of International Economic Development relating more particularly to competition laws and that there is an need to shift the focus from curbing monopolies to promoting competition. With this objective Parliament has taken steps to enact an Act called Competition Act 2002. This is yet to become a part of the statute book but it is certain that it will be replacing the MRTP Act, 1969 in near future

Comparative Provisions of Unfair Trade Practice in other Countries

It is a well established principle of jurisprudence that for every wrong there must be a remedy "*Ubi Jus Ibid Remedium*". All over the world this principle has been recognized and applied to enable an aggrieved party to seek remedy for being compensated for loss or damage suffered by him at the hands of other. Thus Section 82 of the Unfair Trade Practices Act, 1974 of Australia provides that a person who suffers loss or damages by conduct of a person, who is in violation of the provisions relating to restrictive or unfair trade practices, may recover the amount of loss/damages by action against that other person. Section 6 of the Clayton Act and Section 77 of the Sherman Act in United States of America also provides for similar relief. The Combines Investigation Act of Canada also provides by Section 31, the right of any party to recover damages from the person who has indulged in trade practice which are prohibited.[18]

Concluding Remarks

We have discussed about the origin of Unfair Trade Practice in India with the relevant provisions in MRTP Act, 1969 and Consumer Protection Act, 1986, analysis of the definition and discussion of the latest decided cases goes to show the position of the consumers in India who are easily carried away when goods or services are being offered at a discounted rate or when an offer "buy one get one free" is made or for example the prizes are offered under various schemes like scratch and win, play a win etc.

Consumerism is in its infancy in India. It is slowly developing. Apathy of consumers has slackened the growth of consumerism. Many consumers just do not know the legislations available in our country. For instance vegetable oil should be sold in kilograms selling the same in liters is an offence. But common traders sell Edible Oil in liters. Depending on the type of oil sold the consumer may lose 100 to 150 grams for the price he pays per kilogram of oil if the same is given in liters. Though some people know they are not showing interest to exercise their right. In the same way many are not aware about the quality marks, expiry date, etc.

"*It is not the good law, that is important, but it is good administrators*"

"*The success of any law depends on the actual participation of its beneficiaries*".

To quote the words of Pandit Nehru,

"*Laws and Constitution do not by themselves make a country great. It is the enthusiasm, energy and constant effort of the people that make it a great nation*".

Therefore, still consumers understand or made to understand about their rights and responsibilities it is futile to think of a real Consumer Movement.

NOTES

1. (1991) 72 Comp. Cus 702 MRTPC.
2. Subs. by Act 50 of 1993, Section 2 (w.e.f. 18-6-93).
3. Inserted by Act 62 of 2002, Section 2 (w.e.f. 15-3-2002).
4. Inserted by Act 62 of 2002, Section 2 (w.e.f. 15-3-2002).
5. (1989) 3 Section 251.
6. 1 (1992) CPJ 269 (270, 271) (AP).
7. Director Mary Queen's Hospital *vs*. M.J. Jose, II (1999) CPJ 57 (Kerala).
8. S. Ajit *vs*. Dr. M.R. Sreedharan Nair, 1998 (2) CPR 32 (Kerala).
9. Maruti Udyog Ltd. *vs*. Joginder Nath Bhatia, I (2000) CPJ 36 (M.P).
10. H.M. Nazir *vs*. A. Narayanan Nair, II (2003) CPJ 188 (Kerala).
11. 2005 TNCR November 91-92 NCDRC.
12. 12 2004 T.N.C.R Sep-Oct 115-117 SCDRC.
13. 2005 T.N.C.R December 285-288 SCDRC.
14. 2005 T.N.C.R October 199-204 SCDRC.
15. 2005 T.N.C.R. July 1-4 MRTP.
16. 2004 T.N.C.R. (April, May, June) 71-73 SCDRC.
17. 2004 T.N.C.R. November 139-149 SCDRC.
18. www.consumeronline.org.

PART II

Services in Education

Chapter 6

Issues in Higher Educational Service and Consumer Redressal Mechanism

D. RUDRAPPAN

Knowledge is power and knowledge comes through a well-defined educational vision and perception. Greater the expansion of higher education, broader shall be the framework of the national knowledge base and consequently higher the levels of creation and application of that knowledge for the benefit of all. India's achievements in the field of agricultural production, scientific and technological advancements and the breakthroughs in the field of information and communication technology are a clear testimony to the same. Education, particularly higher education imparts ample knowledge and strategy for solving the problems of human beings connected with industry, agriculture, trade, commerce, administration, culture and for improving the quality of overall environment.

After the advent of New Economic Policy initiated in India since 1991, structural adjustment programme followed by the Government laid emphasis on the development of primary education alone leaving higher education at the mercy of private educational barons. The policy of withdrawing slowly from the public higher education system and increasing private participation in higher education is considered not conducive for the development of the nation, economically, socially, politically and educationally as witnessed in Latin American countries and Philippines. Therefore, in this context, the need of the hour is increased public participation in higher educational system. Further, for the smooth development of society, it is not only essential to develop primary education and secondary education but also public higher education for rapid sustainable development.

Vital Role of Higher Education

Kothari Commission on Education, 1966 visualized higher education as an instrument of national development. Higher education ought to be an instrument of promotion of:

(a) Universal values such as Humanism, Tolerance and Universal reason,
(b) National ethos and culture which are also compatible with modern constitutional values,
(c) Expected changes in social, economic, political and civic life in a metamorphic and transitional, contemporary (Indian) society,
(d) Excellence in all works of national life,
(e) Social mobility of large cross-sections of deprived populations,
(f) Manpower requirements of a society on the road to modernization and industrialization, and
(g) Promotion of a culture of 'good life' and a 'good society' as well as 'good governance'.

Mark Blaug explains the importance and value of higher education from the economic, sociological and psychological angle and points out in his monologue that highly educated people are more productive. Further, he adds that employers pay highly educated people more, because they are more achievement motivated, are more self-reliant, act with greater initiative in problem-solving situations, adapt themselves more easily to changing circumstances and assume supervisory responsibilities more quickly. Besides, he has also listed some of the widely held shibboleths about the role of education in the context of the employment problem of the country also. As money incurred in higher education is a social investment, it renders people more productive and increases the volume of employment. Consequently, in the long run, education works to eliminate poverty directly via controlling the growth rate of population and indirectly via an increase in the period for which children are dependent on their parents. And the lower the rate of population growth, the higher the level of income per head.

The educational scenario in the twenty-first century is marked by a distinct shift in approach to quality concerns and development paradigms especially relating to higher education in India. With the advent of globalization in the early 1990's, the challenges of higher education have attained menacing proportions. In the absence of proper body for monitoring effectively the development and quality of higher education in the post-reform period, a number of problems have cropped up. The issues include the pressing need for improvement of quality of higher education, equalization of education access and opportunities to all, proliferation of private higher educational institutions, absence of uniform development of higher education all over the country and the issue of improper coordination among the national bodies of higher education such as All India Council of Technical Education, Medical Council of India and National Council for Teachers Education resulting in unnecessary court disputes. Though Kothari Education Commission (1966) has recommended allocation of 6 per cent of GNP for educational expenditure, the sum allocated by the Government of India remained less than 4 per cent even after 20 years of recommendation. It is pathetic to know that the combined total expenditure of central and state governments on education has declined from 14 per cent in 1980's to 11 per cent in 2000-01. As a proportion of GNP, public expenditure on higher education has declined from 0.95 per cent in 1980-81 to 0.55 per cent in 1989-90 and then to 0.40 per cent in 2004-05.

Instead of opening new state-funded institutions of higher education, the government has permitted more than three thousand so called self-financing institutions all over the country. Rules for granting deemed university status to existing and new institutions have been relaxed by the UGC so that these institutions are outside the control of any affiliating university. The only policy of these institutions is profit making rather than quality education. In a few years from now, self-financing institutions would outnumber the state-funded institutions. Therefore, there is no basis for these private higher educational institutions particularly deemed universities for the collection of heavy amount in the name of capitation fee, donation and exorbitant tuition fees. Another clause of GATS emphasizes transparency in all the functions of educational service. Unfortunately, this clause is followed more in violation of the clause by the private educational barons. No transparency is witnessed in the collection of capitation fee, tuition fee and donations and even in the ownership of educational institutions. Under benami names, politicians and unscrupulous elements own many of these educational institutions. Further, predatory and powerful Trans National Corporations are targeting education, particularly higher education for profit making.

Consumer Redressal Mechanism in Higher Education

The Consumer Protection Act, 1986 ensures the maintenance of satisfactory standards relating to goods and services. National Commission established under the Act has said that it is yet to examine the question, whether educational services come under the purview of consumer courts. Meanwhile, Calcutta and Madras High Courts have categorically held that educational institutions do not come under the ambit of consumer courts. In this scenario, Ministry of Consumer Affairs Government of India has incorporated certain amendments to this Act removing the deficiency relating to service sector.

Before this, Monopolies Restricted Trade Practices Commission which was created by MRTP Act, 1969 has held in the year 1988 that education was service covered when the regulatory control of MRTP Commission. However, later in 1998, a full bench of MRTP Commission has held that education was not a service in the case of Holy Angels School. In the place of MRTP Commission and MRTP Act, Competition Act 2002 has been enacted paving way for the constitution of Competition Commission in the year 2002. The section dealing with definition of the Competition Act, 2002 states:

(u) "Service" means of any description which is made available to potential users and include the provision of service in connection with business of any industrial (or) commercial matters such as banking, communication, education, financing, insurance, real estate, transport etc.

Both educational institutions and the consumers of educational services must take note of the above developments. Institutions should realize that imposing high cost in the consumer for their educational services would no longer be allowed. In 2003, there was a landmark judgment including services in this Act. Therefore, the consumers can resort to court action under the Competition Act, which is not only an inexpensive process but also an effective one. Further, judgment will force institutions to derive quality educational services; otherwise, if there is any deficiency in service for which the consumers paid a price, the consumer can go to a consumer court demanding compensation for the deficiency of educational service. Therefore, educational institutions have to be much more accountable than ever before for delivering quality educational service, keeping up their promises.

Dwelling at length on the present predicament and the persisting challenges of higher education, the paper has hinted at the dwindling financial support by the government and consequent drive for commercialization of higher education by educational barrens besides emphasizing on protection of consumers in higher education and the available mechanism for redressal of deficiency of educational service in terms of Competition Act, 2002.

PART III

Services in Health

Chapter 7

Consumer Rights in Health Sector

S. MARCELIN PUSHPA

"Consumerism" is likely to dominate the Indian market in the next Millennium. The transition will be from a predominantly "sellers market" to a "buyers market" where the choice exercised by the consumer will be influenced by the level of consumer awareness achieved. By "consumerism" we mean the process of realizing the rights of the consumer as envisaged in the Consumer Protection Act (1986) and ensuring right standards for the goods and services for which one makes a payment. This objective can be achieved in a reasonable time frame only when all concerned act together and play their role. The players are the consumers represented by different voluntary non-government consumer organizations, the government, the regulatory authorities for goods and services in a competitive economy, the consumer courts, organizations representing trade, industry and service providers, the law-makers and those in charge of implementation of the laws and rules.

The consumer movement in India is as old as trade and commerce. In Kautilya's *Arthashastra*, there are references to the concept of consumer protection against exploitation by the trade and industry, wrong weights and measures, adulteration and punishment for these offences. However, there was no organized and systematic movement actually safeguarding the interests of the consumers. Prior to independence, the main laws under which the consumer interests were considered were the Indian Penal Code, Agricultural Production, Grading and Marketing Act, 1937; Drugs and Cosmetics Act, 1940. Even though different parts of India exhibited different levels of awareness, in general, the level of awareness was pretty low.

An average Indian consumer is noted for his patience and tolerance. Perhaps because of these superstitious beliefs he considers the receipt of defective goods and services as an act of fate or unfavourable planetary position in his horoscope. When a new television or refrigerator purchased by him turns out to be defective day one, he takes it reticently, blaming it on his fate or as the consequence of the wrongs committed by him in his previous birth. Very often he is exploited, put to avoidable inconveniences and suffers financial loss. It is rather paradoxical that the customer is advertised as the "king" by the seller and service provider; but in actual practice treated as a slave or servant.

Consumer Protection Act, 1986

The issues relating to consumer welfare affects the entire country since everyone is a consumer in one way or the other. Ensuring consumer welfare is the responsibility of the government. Accepting this, policies have been framed and the Consumer Protection Act, 1986, was introduced. A separate Department of Consumer Affairs was also created in the Central and State Governments to exclusively focus on ensuring the rights of consumers as enshrined in the Act. This Act has been regarded as the most progressive, comprehensive and unique piece of legislation. The special feature of this Act is to provide speedy and inexpensive redressal to the grievance of the consumer and provide him relief of a specific nature and award compensation wherever appropriate. The aim of the Act is also to ensure the rights of the consumer, viz. the right of choice, safety, information, redressal, public hearing and consumer education.

The Act defines the consumer as one who purchases goods and services for his/her use. The user of such goods and service with the permission of the buyer is also a consumer. However, a person is not a consumer if he purchases goods and services for resale purpose.

The most important feature of the Act is the provision for setting up a three-tier quasi-judicial machinery popularly known as "consumer courts" at national, state and district levels. The apex court, National Commission functions in Delhi. Every State Government has a State Commission. The third tier is in each district and is called district forum.

Consumer Redress in the Health Sector in India

Despite many reports in the popular press in India about the plight of health care consumers and the implementation of the Consumer Protection Act of 1986, until recently there was very little information about the current system of redress in the health sector in India. A large communication gap had been created between health service providers and patients in India by the enactment of the Consumer Protection Act in 1986 and its implementation in the health services sector. Consumer organizations in India initiated a national campaign to convince public services to publish charters for their users. The Government of India subsequently directed all government utilities to draw up such charters in consultation with their users and with consumer groups.

There is a need to increase the voice of communities in the management of health services which is of utmost importance. A participatory approach to health administration requires instituting a system whereby those who benefit from the services play an active role in ensuring that the system is functioning efficiently. An effective redress mechanism gives consumers a platform for complaining when the system does not work as it should, with the power to rectify inefficiencies and mistakes.

Unlike in industrial countries, where the mechanisms of consumer redress are an integral part of the civic rights tradition, the subject of consumer redress is a relatively new concept in India, particularly in the health sector. The passage of the Consumer Protection Act of 1986 was a first step toward establishing such a tradition in India, in that the legislation empowered consumers to question and challenge the quality of the services they received. However, the deterioration of health care services coupled with a general lack of accountability of providers toward consumers brought home to policy-makers the need to build a permanent system of redress in the health sector. The judgment by the State Commission of Orissa in *Smt. Sukanti Behera vs. Dr. Sashi Bhusan Rath* (1993) upholding the rights of patients to challenge the quality of health care services was a landmark in the history of consumer redress in India. Until then, the medical profession had generally resisted acknowledging that medical services came within the purview of the broader provisions of the Consumer Protection Act. The judgment by the Supreme Court in the *Indian Medical Association vs. V. P. Shantha* (1995) settled the matter by explicitly including medical services in the protections embodied by the Consumer Protection Act.

In accordance with the judgment delivered in *Indian Medical Association vs. V. P. Shantha*, the right to challenge the quality of health care services extends to (a) all patients who pay for services (those in the second category), and (b) all patients who receive free services from institutions that otherwise charge for their services (those in the third category). The Supreme Court ruling excluded the first category from the purview of the Consumer Protection Act of 1986.

The Supreme Court judgment made it clear that losses or damages caused by a deliberate act of negligence, unfair trade practices, or a sub-standard quality of service provided free in India either by the government or by the private sector cannot be challenged under the Consumer Protection Act. This judgment worried consumer organizations because it meant that the poor and disadvantaged consumers who received free health care were open to exploitation and to sub-standard services without having any mechanism for seeking redress. According to the judgment, the only consumers who had a right to seek redress and compensation were those who had paid for their health services. To circumvent this ruling and make all citizens eligible for redress, health care user groups decided to introduce user fees for all health care services in India but to offer free or subsidized services to poor and disadvantaged consumers.

Objectives and Methodology

This chapter addressed three key questions:

- What is the current state of patient redress mechanisms in place at different types of health facilities, both in the public and private sectors?
- What is the current situation regarding the adjudication of problems between consumers and medical providers in various consumer forums established under the Consumer Protection Act?
- What are the legal and administrative impediments to providing speedy, credible, and inexpensive redress to aggrieved patients, and what options are available to improve the situation?

For conceptual clarity, the study chose to review the current system from essentially three viewpoints: (a) the institutional view at the hospital level, (b) the legal view from the consumer forums, and (c) the personal view of the consumer. The chapter examined the procedures that had been adopted at health care facilities to respond to consumers' concerns and complaints. It also assessed the utility and effectiveness of different forums established under the Consumer Protection Act to pay compensation to aggrieved consumers for deliberate acts of negligence that had caused loss or damage to the patient. It took into consideration the perspectives of the consumers, the providers, and the law and reviewed the outcomes of medical negligence cases in legal and statutory (medical councils) systems.

Summary of Cases taken up for Study:

CASE 1

CASE NO.: 443 OF 1997: DISTRICT FORUM, CHENNAI

Case of the Complainant

The child Rahima Begum had fever and coughs and was taken to the opposite party on 21st February 1997. The doctor prescribed tablets, one of which was "Pyrolfin", for two days and also advised the child to conduct blood and urine test. The results of the blood and urine tests proved negative for clinical malaria. Though, the temperature came down, the child developed deep ulceration and fleshy lumps under tongue, puffy eyelids, extensive reddish skin, loss of sensation of both upper and lower limbs, falling hair and loss of appetite. She was under the treatment of the doctor till 3rd March and then was rushed to Kalyani General Hospital. From there she was advised to get admit herself in Child Trust Hospital. The child got herself admitted in Child Trust Hospital on 6th March and was there for nearly 25 days. The complainant reliably understood that the child had developed Stevens-Johnson syndrome, which was due to administering "Pyrolfin" tablets which contained sulpha drug which was allergic to the child. The allegation of the complainant is that the doctor was negligent in not conducting the test to see whether the sulpha drug was allergic to the child or not. The complainant also alleged that child lost one year of schooling and had to be under treatment. The vision of the child is impaired and requires treatment by ophthalmologist and the child was left with ugly scars. The complainant claimed Rs. 26,077.75 towards medical expenses, Rs. 10,000 towards future medical expenses and Rs. 4 lakh towards psychic and physical trauma.

Version of the Opposite Party

The doctor's defence was that the child came with fever, cough and chillness. He suspected it may be "clinical malaria" and had advised the child to conduct blood and urine test. He had by way of caution prescribed citamycin 250 mg (3); malidens (2) and Pyrolfin (2) to the child. The doctor's contention is that he has been practicing medicine for 18 years. The Pyrolfin is a universally accepted drug and also approved by WHO. Since, the child developed Stevens-Johnson's syndrome, the doctor advised the complainant to take the child to Child Trust Hospital, which is well equipped to treat the disease. But the complainant had taken the child to Kalyani General Hospital and from there she was taken to Child Trust when it was felt by the doctor's of Kalyani General Hospital that they did not have the expertise to treat the child. In fact, there was breach of contract. The other contention of the doctor is that the complainant was not kept abreast of the developments and he was kept at dark and the contention of the complainant that the child was under the treatment of the doctor till 3rd March was denied. The doctor denied that there is no test that can be conducted for such sulpha drugs and it is for the patient to disclose if they are allergic to such drug. The doctor denied of any negligence on his part and had claimed Rs. 10,000 as exemplary costs against the complainant.

Finding of the Forum

The forum after giving opportunity to both the sides and after looking into the documents produced by both the parties came to the conclusion that there was no negligence or deficiency on the part of the doctor while administering treatment to the child. It held that the doctor had prescribed the medicine by way of caution and from the literature submitted by the doctor it is seen that the drug is universally accepted drug for curing clinical malaria.

Hence, the Forum dismissed the complaint without costs.

CASE 2

CASE NO.: OP 1004 OF 1998: DISTRICT FORUM, CHENNAI

Case of the Complainant

Lured by the advertisement in Vijay TV about curing of back pain, the complainant went to the opposite party, as he is a naturopathy expert and had assured to cure the complainant within 15 days. On advise the complainant got him admitted on 16.5.1998 and paid Rs. 100 as consultation charges, Rs. 2000 for admission charges and Rs. 500 for petty expenses. On 18.5.1998, three persons came and asked the complainant to do an exercise called "Suthavajnasanam". As the complainant was not able to do the same, the Opposite party asked his subordinates, who have pulled down the body back and put on flat position over the legs and the Opposite party himself sat on the complainant's thighs and due to brutal and uncivilized method of treatment the complainant developed pain and could not raise his leg. He developed bi-lateral foot drop and not able to walk. Within short moment there was numbness below the waist and the complainant could not raise his lower limbs. The opposite party started giving Neurobion Forte and Voverion injection with some ayurvedic injection.

The complainant was advised to use Iodex spray to control the pain. He was carried by attendants and used bed pans for nature calls. The Opposite party advised X-ray and doctor who took X-ray advised correction by means of clinical treatment. He was injected with osteosclerosis due to brutal method used by the Opposite party. On 26.5.1998 and 13.6.1998 the opposite party collected Rs. 2000 thus totalling to Rs. 10,000. The complainant was forced to undergo some surgical operation and after discharge the complainant reached MIOT hospital for special treatment and is still under constant physiotherapy. The Opposite party is using allopathic medicine though he is not authorized to do so.

The complainant is 29 years old and was made immobile and was not able to join his job where he was getting a monthly salary of Rs. 10,000. Hence, the complainant claimed for refund of Rs. 10,000, Rs. 50,000 towards medical expenses, Rs. 50,000 towards travel expenses, Rs. 1 lakh as compensation and Rs. 1000 towards costs.

Version of the Opposite Party

The Opposite party is a qualified doctor in the field of naturopathy. The complainant stayed in the Opposite party's hospital between 16.5.1998 to 13.6.1998. He voluntarily got himself discharged on 13.6.1998. The opposite party never promised of any cure within 15 days. The Opposite party never administered any injection. The complainant was referred to M.R. Hospital for X-ray to see the progress after treatment and not as alleged by the complainant. As the progress was slow he was advised to continue the treatment at home. He was walking briskly when he was discharged. Hence, there was no negligence or deficiency on the part of the opposite party.

Finding of the Forum

After considering the arguments of both the parties the Forum held that no expert opinion or evidence was let in by the complainant that the treatment given by the opposite party was the cause for the disease called osteosclerosis or numbness. Similarly, no evidence was given to show that the opposite party had made any promise to cure the illness within 15 days. The complainant has not produced contra-evidence to show that he having taught "Suthavarjasanam". He did not file any rejoinder to deny that he walked briskly when he was discharged. The Forum further held that "perhaps the slow development had made the complainant to file this case. Therefore, the complaint is liable to be dismissed. The complaint is dismissed."

CASE 3
CASE NO: 241 OF 2001: DISTRICT FORUM, CHENNAI

Case of the Complainant

The complainant, Dilshad Fathima, filed a complaint against N.R. Medical Home and Dr.(Mrs.) Nasreen Ahmed (gynecologist). The case of the complainant is that she had delivered a third girl baby on 7th April 1999 and thereafter underwent a sterilization operation. On 21st June 2001 she met Dr. Nasreen as she was having nausea and vomiting. The doctor informed her that she was pregnant again. The complainant was shocked to know this. Later in October 2001 the complainant filed a case against the hospital and the doctor claiming

Rs. 6000 towards reimbursement of expenses of delivery of the third child; Rs. 50,000 towards deficiency of service by the opposite parties in failing to perform proper sterilization; Rs. 1 lakh compensation for mental agony and Rs. 5000 as costs of the complaint, thus totalling to Rs. 1.61 lakh.

Version of the Opposite Party

The version of the Opposite parties was that the complainant was performed sterilization adopting "Pomeroy's" technique. And according to this practice there is a 0.2 to 1 per cent failure. The parties also contended that the failure was not an immediate one but the complainant had become pregnant after a lapse of nearly 2 years. Hence, no negligence can be attributed to the doctor. It was also contended that the complainant was offered an option of terminating the pregnancy and re-sterilization free of cost when she came on 21st June, 2001. But she opted to continue the pregnancy saying that the fourth child may turn out to be a male child.

Finding of the Forum

The Forum after hearing the arguments of both the counsels appearing on behalf of the complainant and the opposite parties and after going through the documents filed by both the parties and taking into consideration the judgements already passed by various State and National Commission on similar facts came to the conclusion that there was no negligence on the part of the doctor and the hospital and had dismissed the complaint.

CASE 4
APPEAL NOs.: 61 OF 1999 AND 171 OF 2002: STATE COMMISSION, CHENNAI.

Complainant's Case

Mrs Thulasimani had some gynecological disorders. She was advised removal of her uterus by surgery. On 30.4.1996 the surgery was performed. On 7.5.1996, the complainant's wife passed away at Coimbatore Kidney Centre. The death certificate issued mentioned that the death was due to acute renal failure and septicemia. Septicemia is a condition when bacteria or fungi actually multiplying in the blood usually with the production of severe symptoms such as fever and hypertension. It develops from unclean and septic gadgets, theatre, catheters such as intravenous peritoneal, urinary wound infection and deep infection may also bring septicemia. Since operation the complainant's wife had discomfort and uneasiness. This was informed to the Opposite party.

The complaint alleged negligence on the part of the Opposite party for the following reasons: the opposite party failed to keep the gadgets in an aseptic condition, contradictions in nurses notes and doctor's case sheet, administration of steriod (decadron) even after diagnosing septicemia, failure of information to the deceased's relatives about the patient's condition, failure to exercise due care and caution by permitting inappropriate experts to deal with the case and failed to exercise due care and caution through surgery and thereafter.

On 17.5.1996, the complainant's counsel called for the case records from the opposite party's hospital. The Opposite party gave the case sheet and nurses notes through their counsel after a delay of 26 days. In the reply notice dated 10.6.1996, the opposite party conceded that the patient developed complications while still under treatment. The complainant claimed Rs. 5 lakh as compensation for the deficiency in service by the opposite party.

Opposite Party's Version

The complainant had already filed OP 143 of 1996 and was dismissed for default. On 12.3.1997, the complainant filed a restoration application and the same was dismissed on merits. Hence, the principle of *res judicata* (the court shall not entertain a case which has already been decided on the same issue between the same parties arising on same cause of action) would apply. Before coming to the opposite party's hospital, the lady was examined by Dr. Shyamala, leading gynecologist for excessive discharge during menstrual periods and Dr. Shyamala advised removal of uterus and was referred to the opposite party. Previously the lady's sister Saraswathi was successfully operated by the opposite party for a similar problem. The complainant's wife got admitted and was operated upon on 30.4.1996. The opposite party had used all well sterilized and bacteria-free materials. Almost two operations are performed daily and no complaints have been reported so far. It may be due to very low immunity of the patient that even a small infection could have caused septicemia. On 30.4.1996 and 1.5.1996, she was on intravenous ailment. On 2nd and 3rd May, she was on oral food and on 4th on solid food. Since she complained vomiting and giddiness on 5th, she was attended by Dr. Elango M.D. on 5th, 6th and 7th and the patient was discharged. Dr. Elango suspected septicemia and gave all antibiotics. On 6th, Dr. Elango called Dr. P.N. Shanmugam, urologist, to rule out the problems in the kidney. Dr. Shanmugam examined her and found urinal output was normal and advised continuation of the same treatment. On 7th the opposite party contacted Dr. K.S. Ramalingam of Coimbatore Kidney Centre over phone and on his advice the complainant's wife was sent to Coimbatore after discharging her. She was sent in a well-equipped ambulance. A qualified nurse also accompanied her. Hence, there was no negligence on the part of the opposite party.

District Forum's Finding: (*Erode*)

Exhibits 20 to 22 and B7 would go to show that the complainant filed a memo in the district forum on 27.4.1998 stating that he has filed an appeal before the State Commission to set aside the order of dismissal for default in OP 148/96. On 21.11.1998, the complainant had sent a letter to withdraw the appeal as trial in this case has been taken up. On 25.1.1999, the appeal was withdrawn in the State Commission. Hence, principle of *res judicata* would not apply.

After considering the facts of the case and arguments put forth by both the parties and from the fact that the nurses have administered some other medicines which were not prescribed by the doctors, the President of the district forum came to the conclusion that the complainant is entitled to Rs. 4.50 lakh as compensation for loss of his wife.

On the contrary, the members of the district forum held that there were no negligence on the part of the opposite party and dismissed the complaint with compensatory costs of Rs. 5000 to be paid by the complainant to the Opposite party.

State Commission's Finding

Hence, two appeals arose from the judgments passed in the district forum. AP 61 of 1999 was filed by the complainant against the majority order passed by the non-judicial members and AP 171 of 2002 was filed by the opposite party against the order of the judicial member (president) of the forum. Mr. R. Gandhi, senior advocate, advanced arguments on behalf the complainant and Mr. K. Duraiswamy, senior advocate, argued for the opposite party. The State Commission held that the principle of *res judicata* shall not apply as the original case (OP 148/96) was not decided on merits. It also held that the majority order of the forum below is not sustainable in law and hence, the order of the President was upheld. In substance, AP 61 of 1999 was allowed upholding the President's order and AP 171 of 2002 was dismissed setting aside the order of the majority members of the district forum.

CASE 5
CASE NO: OP 105 OF 2000: DISTRICT FORUM, CHENNAI

Complainant's Case

Complainant married Ms. Anupriya on 10.9.1998. In the year 1999, she developed some gynecological problems and hence consulted Dr. Hemalatha, gynecologist. After various tests and ultrasound scan certain medicines were prescribed. She did not get any relief. Again the complainant's wife met Dr. Hemalatha in the last week of August 1999. The doctor advised diagnostic laparoscopy. Ms Anupriya got herself admitted as in-patient in Dr. Mu Va's Hospital on 8.10.1999. After laparoscopy, Anupriya developed breathlessness and became hyposensive and she had to be ventilated immediately. Since the hospital had no ventilator facility, it was brought from outside. She was ventilated and incubated at 03:00 am on 9.10.1999. Later, she was shifted to Soorya Hospital. There without regaining consciousness, Anupriya died at 9:40 pm on 9.10.1999. The complainant alleged spending Rs. 10,000 for various tests between February-September 1999; Rs. 1500 towards medicines and Rs. 50,000 as medical expenses on 8th October 1999; Rs. 10,000 towards the hospital expenses, laboratory tests, doctors fee, medicines, etc. to the third Opposite party.

The complainant further alleged that first Opposite party refused to give case sheet, discharge report, bills for various amounts collected and to furnish the name of the anesthetist or the exact cause for the sudden breathlessness of the complainant's wife. The complainant termed the death certificate issued by the third opposite party as ridiculous and fallacious. Hence, the complainant claimed Rs. 4 lakh as compensation for the death of his wife and Rs. 75,000 towards reimbursement of medical expenses from the first and second opposite parties. There was no claim against the third Opposite party.

Version of 1st Opposite Party

The first opposite party denied running Dr. Mu Va's Hospital. The first opposite party said that she was just a consultant in that hospital. The complainant's wife also consulted for her inability to conceive and infertility. The case of the complainant's wife was a case of primary infertility. Hence, diagnostic laparoscopy was suggested and referred to Dr. Viswanathan Pai, eminent laparascopic surgeon and he performed the same on 8.10.1999 at 8:00 a.m. He was assisted by Dr. Bushanam, senior anesthetist, residing at Anna Nagar, Chennai. She was ventilated with oxygen from Boyles apparatus followed by ventilator. Monitored every 5 minutes till 11:05 p.m and thereafter every 15 minutes till about 7:30 a.m. As she failed to recover from anesthesia, Dr. Geetha Lakshmipathy, M.D., professor of neurology, Kilpauk Medical College, was called. She came early in the morning on 9.10.1999 and saw the patient. Then she suggested shifting the patient to Soorya Hospital. The patient was shifted by ambulance with portable ventilator and pulse oxymeter. At last, the patient died on 9.10.1999 about 10:40 p.m due to hypoxic encephalopathy and brain stem dysfunction resulting in cardio respiratory arrest.

The Opposite party denied having received any fee and performed the laparoscopy free of cost. The opposite party also denied the allegations of negligence on their part.

Version of 3rd Opposite Party

The third Opposite party against whom there was no claim, contended that the patient was seen by the neurologist and neurosurgeon and other doctors. The cause of the death was recorded at the time as "Cardio Respiratory Arrest".

Finding of the Forum

The forum after considering the documents filed and arguments advanced held that complainant has not proved that opposite parties have committed deficiency in service and negligence in their duties and hence is not entitled for compensation. It also held that reasonable care has been taken by the first opposite party.

CASE 6
CASE NO: O.P. NO. 95 OF 1992: DISTRICT FORUM, CHENNAI

Case of the Complainant

K. Vasantha, the complainant a 30 year old woman wanted to have a second child 7 years after her first child. Dr. Lakshmi Dandayudapani prescribed certain costly medicines for improving chances of pregnancy. On 18.02.91, the doctor confirmed that she was pregnant. On 02.03.91, she developed fever and was taken to the opposite party hospital for treatment. She was examined and on 03.03.91, D&C was performed. She continued to have pain and so some medicines were prescribed. There was no improvement and a scan of the pelvis was taken. It was detected to be a case of "missed abortion". The complainant was taken to CMC Vellore for further treatment and a dead foetus was removed from the tube.

The complainants argued that the opposite parties had wrongly done the D&C due to which the foetus was pushed to the tubes. They argued that it was a case of normal pregnancy and due to the wrongly done D&C she had lost her second baby. They had claimed compensation of Rs. 2,19,000 for the loss of child and the medical expenses.

Version of the Opposite Party

The Opposite party doctor argued with a lot of literature on tubal pregnancy and proved that there was no negligence.

Finding of the Court

The court held that there was no negligence or deficiency of service on part of the doctors and the case was dismissed.

Conclusion and Recommendations

The interviews at the hospitals and the accompanying review of medical negligence cases heard at consumer forums have confirmed that there is an urgent and immediate need to reform the present system of consumer redress in the health sector. The findings revealed a disturbing trend of adhoc practices in the management of consumer complaints in the majority of hospitals.

Findings

In-House Complaint Procedures

The study found that most of the hospitals lacked a standardized procedure to handle complaints. It also found some slackness in offering prompt redress for consumers' complaints. The study's review of facilities confirmed that management tends to be inattentive to consumers' concerns.

An inquiry into the nature of complaints lodged revealed that there were surprisingly few complaints relating to clinical services. In the private sector, the largest number of complaints was related to sanitation, followed by complaints about hospital utilities and billing. In the public sector, sanitation was again the most frequent reason for complaint, followed by hospital utilities and medical care. The fact that so few complaints related to the quality of clinical services in both the public and the private sectors may have reflected consumers' limited knowledge, low expectations of the quality of health services, or management's denial of clinical problems. The private sector appears to be more adept than its public counterpart in terms of how it handles complaints.

Big hospitals have established mechanisms for settling disputes; smaller hospitals resolve disputes primarily through informal means. However, in both large and small hospitals, the present system offers no concrete guarantees to the complainants that the authorities would actually address their problems within a specified time frame. The absence of a fixed period for resolving disputes inevitably meant that most cases were either resolved almost immediately or were left unresolved. It is significant that consumers found the unresponsive attitude of the hospital authorities to be one of the main factors that prompted them to take their grievances to the courts.

Concerning the functioning of consumer forums, it is noteworthy that the majority of both consumers and providers described their experiences as largely negative. Prolonged litigation due to recurring delays was cited as one of the major shortcomings of the process. Most felt that the present infrastructure for consumer redress was highly inadequate—"too few forums for the number of cases." In 90 per cent of the cases, the time taken to resolve the conflict went well beyond the stipulated period of 90 days. Most complainants named this long waiting period as the most trying aspect of the litigation process.

Another negative aspect of the current system is its overdependence on lawyers. The providers were better equipped legally than the consumers in that they had their own legal staff to fight their cases, but the majority of consumers also engaged lawyers to help them.

A third aspect of the functioning of courts relates to the subject of compensation. At present, there are no guidelines that govern the sums to be awarded, which means in practice that most compensation is limited to the price of the medical service provided. However, in cases of medical negligence where a severe disability or even death is the main focus, awarding only enough to cover the costs of the patient's medical services is likely to leave the complainant feeling highly dissatisfied. In order to restore credibility to the system, the compensation policy needs to be reviewed.

Even more important than compensation is the question of access. As the study revealed, access to Consumer Courts is largely restricted to people who have a regular source of income. The rural and urban poor, scheduled castes and tribes, and women are underrepresented among complainants and consequently have little effective voice in the management of health services throughout the country.

Recommendations for Increasing the Efficiency of Consumer Forums

The study recommends the gradual and steady incorporation of certain measures into the existing system of consumer redress in the Indian health sector in the near future.

The development and adoption of a mandatory Citizen's Charter for all hospitals that clearly highlights the rights of patients vis-à-vis the hospital authorities in the delivery of health services. This charter must be made available to all patients at all times and in the language in which they normally communicate, with special emphasis on illiterate and disadvantaged consumers.

The study suggests that the service provider in question should handle complaints within the health care sector professionally. In both private and public health facilities, management should be able to deal with customer complaints more effectively by providing a written manual that gives specific directions for filing a complaint and a time frame for such action to consumers who want to make a complaint. The names of the personnel who handle complaints should be prominently displayed to ensure that they are accountable to the consumers. Government should provide resources to fund skill development programmes to train these personnel in customer care and effective communication. At the moment, very little attention is given to human resource development in either the public or the private sectors.

The Government of India also needs to improve the infrastructure of the Consumer Forums. Most of the cases filed in the Consumer Courts take more than the stipulated 90 days to be resolved. To reduce the pressure on individual courts and ensure a speedy trial to consumers, it is absolutely necessary to increase the number of District Forums and State Commissions throughout the country, proportionate to the regions' populations. Every two to three years, the Ministry of Consumer Affairs should make a standard assessment of whether the District Forums are functioning effectively to buttress the system's credibility and to ensure that redress is being provided promptly.

The need to increase public awareness of consumer issues is another key recommendation. Consumer redress in the health sector in India, as elsewhere, is intrinsically influenced by overall consumer awareness. However, the fact that only those who approached the courts had been influenced by consumer organizations and only by the media shows that both consumer organizations and the media must focus more on generating awareness of the redress system. Having this information will empower consumers, which in turn will lead them to demand high quality health care services.

As pointed out above, the survey highlighted the overwhelming level of consumer dependence on lawyers in the Consumer Forum system. Many of the lawyers interviewed claimed to be working on more than 50 consumer cases at a time. Such a high level of dependence not only makes the whole procedure of redress expensive, but it also significantly reduces the contribution of the consumer in the redress process. The Consumer Protection Act of 1986 has already gone through two amendments to make it more effective and pro-consumer. This study recommends that the Consumer Protection Act and the Indian Medical Council (IMC) Act of 1956 be amended to bring all medical practitioners and health care services, whether in the public or the private sectors, within the purview of the accountability and compensation aspects of the law.

This would definitely benefit the average Indian consumer. A large number of poor people visit government hospitals, and the present legal situation in effect prevents them from challenging the quality of health care services they receive. The Constitution of India guarantees equality to all citizens, yet the present Consumer Protection Act actually introduces an element of inequality among patients, because private patients are covered by the Act while public patients are not. A more serious concern is that this restriction also reduces the general accountability of hospitals to their patients and, since the poor depend on government hospitals for inpatient services, in effect prevents the poor from having full basic citizenship rights.

Every citizen should have access to high-quality health care services and be able to claim compensation for deliberate acts of negligence or for unfair trade practices. The laws should also cover doctors working in government hospitals and charitable institutions. The Consumer Protection (Amendment) Bill, which is currently awaiting parliamentary approval, will cover services such as health and medical services and also mandatory services provided by central and state governments.

Consumer complainants have tended to find themselves in a disadvantageous position compared with doctors. While doctors are always well equipped with all the documentary evidence that they need from the hospital records, the complainants often find it difficult to muster the necessary evidence to prove their cases. Therefore, in many past cases, the complainants were not able to prove medical negligence beyond a reasonable doubt. This is one of the reasons why the IMC Act has been inadequate in dealing with medical negligence and why the consumer forums have become more popular. Moreover, doctors are generally reluctant to give evidence against their professional colleagues, even in instances of genuine malpractice, in cases involving the IMC. This has prompted some consumer advocates to recommend ways to improve the IMC Act.

Ensuring consumer redress for medical mistakes and malpractice is an important component of a larger push toward democratizing health management. As consumers' awareness of their rights increases, this provides a fertile ground in which to plant the seeds of a broader consumer movement in the health sector in India.

This study has brought to light how existing structures for handling complaints work in both private and public sector health care institutions and has suggested various possible solutions for building a strong and dependable infrastructure in the health sector in India. If providers were to benchmark the quality of services that they provide and improve the existing system of health care management they might avoid much dissatisfaction and many complaints from consumers. Policy-makers would have to develop such an initiative in consultation with service providers, users, consumer groups, and the government agencies that deal with health care delivery.

However, not all of the signs are negative. The existing legal framework for protecting and compensating consumers in the health sector has some encouraging aspects. It has established the fact that well-designed legislation can build awareness among consumers and generate demand for high-quality services, although in the area of medical care there is a long way to go. Civil society in India will not soon forget the uproar made by medical practitioners when the Supreme Court of India brought doctors under the provisions of the Consumer Protection Act, thus making them accountable to patients.

It is interesting to note that in spite of U.N. recognition, encouragement from the developed countries and the pro-active role played by the Government, the consumer in India still does not get his due. It is time that he wakes up and realizes his rights. It will be useful if voluntary consumer organizations take up this role and make way for the realization of the objectives of the Consumer Protection Act. It is agreed on all hands that "consumer empowerment" in India has a long way to go. This is the right time to act. Let us prepare and usher in a new era of "Consumerism". When we cross the winter, spring cannot be far behind.

REFERENCES

Annoussamy, D. (1999). "Medical Profession and the Consumer Protection Act", *Journal of Indian Law Institute,* Vol. 41(3), pp. 460-466.

Bhat, R. (1986). Regulating the Private Health Care Sector: The Case of the Indian Consumer Protection Act, *Health Policy and Planning,* pp. 265-279.

Consumer Protection Reporter (CPR), 1986.

Goyal, A. (1999). Consumer Protection Act, 1986: Structural Loopholes in Consumer Courts' Constitution—"A Brief Analysis", *Journal of Indian Law Institute,* Vol. 41(2), pp. 273-279.

Misra, B., Kalra, P. (2000). *A Study on the Regulatory Framework for Consumer Redress in the Health Care Sector in India*, conducted by Voluntary Organization in Interest of Consumer Education (VOICE).

Soma, Wadhwa (2001). "Hypocratic Practice", *Outlook Magazine,* 3rd February 2003.

Srivastava, Syed, S.J. (2001). "Legal Framework for Health Care in India: Experience and Future Directions", The Indian Law Institute, *Journal of Indian Law Institute,* Vol. 38 (3), 1996, pp. 377-386.

Chapter 8

Consumer Rights in Service Sectors: Medical Service

P. BRINDA

Introduction

Practice of medicine is as old as existence of human race. Originally, the priest functioned as preacher, teacher, judge as well as healer. He was the first physician and his relationship with his patients was unique and unquestioned. With the passage of time not only has practice of medicine graduated to become independent and noble profession, but his relationship has slowly shifted from 'Next to God' to 'Friend, Philosopher and Guide', to 'respected professional' and, today, to service provider. With increased consumer awareness, rising expectation, western trend of medical liability litigation, Consumer Protection Act, and judicial activism, increasing number of complaints are being filed by dissatisfied patients resulting in growing distrust between patients and doctors and increased cost of medical treatment.

History of Consumer Movement in India

Giving an account of the history of consumer movement in India, the Department of Consumer Affairs in a note furnished to the committee informed that the consumer movement in India is as old as trade and commerce. In Kautilya's *Arthashastra*, there are references to the concept of protection of the consumer against exploitation by trade and industry, short weights and measurements, adulteration and punishment of these offences. However, there was no organized and systematic movement actually safeguarding the interests of the consumers.

Prior to independence, consumer interests were considered mainly under laws like the Indian Penal Code, Agricultural Produce (Grading and Marking Act, 1937), Drugs and Cosmetics Act, 1940 etc. even though, different parts of India had different levels of awareness, in general, the level of awareness was low.

Consumer Protection Act, 1986

Consumer Protection Act, 1986 was enacted to better protect the interest of the consumers. It is one of the most progressive and comprehensive piece of legislation and it is an umbrella legislation covering all goods and services. The Act provides for a separate three-tier quasi-judicial consumer dispute redressal machinery at the National, State and District levels and is intended to provide simple, speedy and inexpensive redressal for consumers' grievances.

For complete understanding of the term 'medical negligence' it would be proper to understand the terms Deficiency, Consumer and Service which have been defined under Sections 2(1)(g), (d) and (o) respectively of the Consumer Protection Act (CP Act).

Definitions

'Deficiency'—Section 2 (1)(g)

"Deficiency" means any fault, imperfection, shortcoming or inadequacy in the quality, nature and manner of performance which is required to be maintained by or under any law for the time being in force or has been undertaken to be performed by a person in pursuance of a contract or otherwise in relation to any services.

Consumer—Section 2(1)(d)

"Consumer" means any person who buys any goods for a consideration which has been paid or promised or partly paid and partly promised, or under any system of deferred payment and includes any user of such goods other than the person who buys such goods for consideration paid or promised or partly paid and partly promised, or under any system of deferred payment when such use is made with the approval of such person, but does not include a person who obtains such goods for resale or for any commercial purpose; or [hires or avails of] any services for a consideration which has been paid or promised or partly paid and partly promised, or under any system of deferred payment and includes any beneficiary of such services other than the person who [hires or avails of] the services for consideration paid or promised, or partly paid and partly promised, or under any system of deferred payment, when such services are availed of with the approval of the first mentioned person [but does not include a person who avails of such services for any commercial purpose].

[*Explanation*: For the purpose of this clause, "commercial purpose" does not include use by a person of goods bought and used by him and services availed by him exclusively for the purposes of earning his livelihood by means of self-employment;]

The section includes any user of goods other than the person who buys such goods when such use is made with the approval of the buyer. A person other than the original party to the transaction who hires any services, that is to say, a beneficiary of those services, can also maintain a complaint under the Act.[1]

Spring Meadows Hospital Case[2]

A child patient was treated for seven days in the Spring Meadows Hospital (Noida) for typhoid. The consultant physician prescribed "Chioromphenical injunction", but the unqualified nurse misread it as "chloroquine" and indented, for the purchase of injection, "Lariago" (i.e. chloroquine). She injected chloroquine 5 mg IV, which was at least 3-1/2 times of the normal pediatric dose. The patient suffered irreversible brain damage. Treatment for 21 days in AIIMS, New Delhi, did not help. The patient was compelled to live in a vegetative state.

The National Commission came to the conclusion that the attending doctor was negligent, as he allowed an unqualified nurse to administer the injection, even though the consultant doctor had advised administration by the attending doctor himself. The judgment was confirmed by the Supreme Court and held that the hospital and the nurse were jointly and severally liable.

Compensation Awarded

Rs. 12.5 lakhs to the child (Rs. 10 lakhs compensation, plus Rs. 2.5 lakhs for equipment) and Rs. 5 lakhs to the parents, for mental agony.

Meaning of the Expression Consumer

The Supreme Court further held that when a young child is taken to a hospital and treated by the hospital, then

(a) The child's parents would come within the definition of "consumer" [Section 2(1)(d)(ii)]; and
(b) The child also becomes a "consumer", being a beneficiary of such services.

[Even where the patient is a married daughter, the parents who are required to spend for her treatment, are also "consumers".[3]

Service—Section 2 (1)(o)

"Service" means service of any description which is available to potential [users and includes, but not limited to, the provision of] facilities in connection with banking, financing, insurance, transport, processing, supply of electrical or other energy, board or lodging or both, [housing construction,] entertainment, amusement or the purveying of news or other information, but does not include the rendering of any service free of charge or under a contract of personal service;

Indian Medical Association *vs.* V. P. Shantha[4]

Though the word services as defined under the CP Act does not specifically include professional services rendered by Doctors, and similarly the word consumer does not specifically cover patients but the National Commission and later the Supreme Court of India in the case of *Indian Medical Association vs. V.P. Shantha*, has held that the services rendered by the medical practitioner is included and covered under the definition of services as per Section 2(1)(o) of the CP Act.

The detailed position is as under:

(i) Where services are rendered free of charge to everyone, the Act does not apply.
(ii) But, where the fees charged are required to be paid by every body availing of the services, then the Consumer Protection Act applies.

Where charges are required to be paid by persons availing of services, but certain categories of persons (who cannot afford to pay) are not charged for services, then also, the Act applies.

Supreme Court's Settled Rule—Medical Services Falls within the Purview of Consumer Protection Act

Compelled by circumstances, different judgments of various courts/ fora, the Indian Medical Association approached Supreme Court *vide* Civil Appeal No. 688/93 and 689/93 along with SLP(s) No. 6885 and 6950 of 92 filed by Cosmopolitan Hospital. The case was finally heard by a "3 Judge Bench" consisting Hon'ble Justices Kuldeep Singh, S.C. Aggarwal and B.L. Hansaria which disposed off all the appeals (group of cases) pending before the Supreme Court relating to Medical Profession and CP Act by its landmark judgment dated 13.11.1995.

The Supreme Court went in depth of the whole issue of *"rendering of services"* and held that the clause applies to "any" services made available to *"potential users"*. The word 'any' has been used in wider sense extending from 'one to all'. Similarly, word "potential user" covers not only actual users but those capable of using or availing. Thus clause 2(1)(o) is very wide and extends to any or all actual or potential users.

Regarding *'contract of personal service'* the learned judges did not agree that 'Doctor-Patient Relationship' cannot be called contract of personal service and be equated to 'Master-Servant relationship'. To some extent he may be servant of society but with society having distrust in paternalistic attitude of doctors—doctor also has little wish to be paternalistic—with commercialization as well as consumerism having entered in medical services, these can at best be regarded as services of personal nature but can't be treated as contract of personal service.

The Supreme Court while delivering judgment on the appeal of IMA and other SLPs and Writ petitions regarding application of Consumer Protection Act to medical professionals on 13th November, 1995 arrived at the following conclusions:

(1) Service rendered to a patient by a medical practitioner (except where the doctor renders service free of charge to every patient or under a contract of personal service), by way of

consultation, diagnosis and treatment, both medicinal and surgical, would fall within the ambit of 'services' as defined in Section 2(1)(o) of the Act.

(2) A 'contract of personal service' has to be distinguished from a 'contract for personal services'. In the absence of a relationship of master and servant between the patient and medical practitioner, the service rendered by a medical practitioner to the patient cannot be regarded as service rendered under a 'contract of personal service'. Such service is service rendered under a 'contract for personal services' and is not covered by exclusionary clause of the definition of 'service' contained in Section 2(1)(o) of the Act.

(3) The expression 'contract of personal service' in Section 2(1)(o) would include the employment of a medical officer for the purpose of rendering medical service to the employer. The service rendered by a medical officer to his employer under the contract of employment would be outside the purview of 'service' as defined in Section.

(4) Service rendered free of charge by a medical practitioner attached to a hospital/nursing home or a medical officer employed in a hospital/nursing home where such services are rendered free of charge to every body, would not be 'service' as defined in Section 2(1)(o) of the Act. The payment of a token amount for registration purpose only at the hospital/nursing home would not alter the position.

(5) Service rendered by a medical practitioner or a hospital/nursing home cannot be regarded as service rendered free of charge, if the person availing the service has taken an insurance policy for medical care where under the charges for consultation, diagnosis and medical treatment are borne by the insurance company and such service would fall within the ambit of 'service' as defined in Section 2(1)(o) of the Act.

(6) As a part of the condition of service, if the employer bears the expenses of medical treatment of an employee and his family members dependent on him, the service rendered to such an employee and his family members by a medical practitioner or a hospital/nursing home would not be free of

charge and would constitute 'service' under Section 2(1)(o) of the Act.

Service Rendered at a Non-government Hospital/Nurshing Home

(7) Where no charge whatsoever is made from any person availing the service and all patients (rich and poor) are given free service is outside the purview of the Section 2(1)(o). The payment of a token amount for registration purpose only at the hospital/nursing home would not alter the position.

(8) Where charges are required to be paid by the persons availing such services falls within the purview of definition 'service'.

(9) Where charges are required to be paid by persons who are in a position to pay and persons who cannot afford to pay are rendered service free of charge would fall within the ambit of the expression 'service' Free service would also be "service" and the recipient a 'consumer' under the Act.

Service Rendered at a Government Hospital/Health Centre/ Dispensary

(10) Where no charge whatsoever is made from any person availing the service and all patients (rich or poor) are given free service is outside the purview of the expression 'service' as defined in Section 2(1)(o) of the Act. The payment of a token amount for registration purpose only at the hospital/ nursing home would not alter the position.

(11) Where services are rendered on payment of charges and also rendered free of charge to other persons availing such services would fall within the ambit of the expression 'service' as defined in Section 2(1)(o) of the Act irrespective of the fact that the service is rendered free of charge to persons who do not pay for such service. Free service would also be 'service' and the recipient a 'consumer' under the Act.

In view of the above conclusions, the Supreme Court dismissed IMA's appeal as well as all other SLPs and Writ Petitions related to these issues and before it.

No "Sovereign Immunity"—Negligence of Government Employees

The judgment of the Supreme Court in *Nilabati Behera's case*[5] holds that in view of the fundamental right to life (Article 21 of the Constitution) the Government cannot claim "sovereign immunity" for liability for the negligence of its employees.

The right to health and health care is protected under Article 21 of the Constitution of India, as a right to life. When doctors performed their duties towards the patient negligently in a Government Hospital, the servants of the state violated the fundamental right of the patient, guaranteed under Article 21 of the Constitution.

By following the principle of law enunciated by the Supreme Court in *Nilabati Behera's case*, the Andhra Pradesh High Court, *Mrs. Shantha vs. State of Andhra Pradesh*[6] exercised its jurisdiction under Article 226 of the Constitution of India (writ jurisdiction) to award compensation to a patient, whose treatment was done negligently by the doctors in a Government Hospital. The High Court directed the State of Andhra Pradesh to pay compensation to the patient for negligent treatment by the doctors employed in the Hospital.

Private Medical Practitioners, Private Nursing Homes and Hospitals—Service—Provided it is not a free Service

State Commission of Maharashtra in the case of *B. Shekhar Hegde vs. Dr. S. Bhattacharya & other*[7] declared that definition of 'services' as provided in CP Act under clause 2(1)(o) includes services rendered by Private Medical Practitioners, Private Nursing Homes and Hospitals provided it is not a free service.

A Division Bench of Madhya Pardesh High Court in the case of *Dr. G.C. Batalia vs. The Consumer Dispute Redressal Forum & other*[8] concurred with the above judgment of Maharashtra State Commission and held that the expression service having been defined under Section 2(1)(o) give such broad language and a widest amplitude and restricting the definition to only services relating to commercial transactions.

Hence, include services rendered by Private Medical Practitioners, Private Hospitals and Nursing Homes, provided it is not a free service".

The National Commission in *M/s. Cosmopolitan Hospital and other vs. Vasantha P. Nair*[9] held that the activity of providing medical assistance for payment carried out by hospitals and members of medical profession falls within the scope of Section 2(1)(o) of the Act. The treatment given was totally free of any charge it did not constitute service as defined under the Act. The National Commission observed that if the treatment given was totally free of any charge it did not constitute service as defined under the Act.[10]

Negligence—Definition and a View

Negligence is the opposite of diligence. An act is said to be performed negligently when it is performed without due diligence. That is to say, that the standard of care exhibited whilst performing the act was below par. When an act is done without the requisite care and caution, the act can be labelled as a rash act. Negligence and rashness usually go hand-in-hand and in general denotes carelessness.

Before the enforcement of the Consumer Protection Act, medical negligence was inevitably governed by the law of torts. The classic attempted judicial definition of negligence is noticed in *Blyth vs. Birmingham Co.* [(1856) 11 Exch 781 784], wherein Alderson B. said: "Negligence is the omission to do something which a reasonable man, guided upon those considerations which regulate the conduct of human affairs would do, or doing something which a prudent and reasonable man would not do." ***Salmond*** in his authoritative treatise on the Law of Torts (19th edition) referred to this definition. Lord Write said: "In strict legal analysis, negligence means more than heedless or careless conduct, whether in omission or commission; it properly connotes the complex concept of duty, breach and damage thereby suffered by the person to whom the duty was owing".

In India as in England, it is well settled that medical malpractice cases are governed by the general principles of law of torts. Negligence has many manifestations—it may be active negligence, collateral negligence, comparative negligence, concurrent negligence, continued negligence, criminal negligence, gross negligence, hazardous negligence, active and passive negligence, willful or reckless negligence, administrative negligence or negligence '*per se*'.

In Black's Law Dictionary negligence '*per se*' is defined as: 'Conduct, whether of action or omission, which may be declared and treated as negligence without any argument or proof as to the particular surrounding circumstances, either because it is in violation of a statute or valid municipal ordinance, or because it is so palpably opposed to the dictates of common prudence that it can be said without hesitation or doubt that no careful person would have been guilty of it. As a general rule, the violation of a public duty, enjoined by law for the protection of person or property, so constitutes."

It was also observed that where a person is guilty of negligence *per se*, no further proof is needed.[11] Negligence therefore consists of two acts. The act of not doing (omitting) something, that a reasonable man, under the circumstances, would do (act of omission); and doing something which a reasonable prudent man under the circumstances would not do (act of commission). An action for negligence proceeds upon the idea of a duty or an obligation on the part of the doctor to use the required care and caution. The breach of this duty may result in injury to the patient.

It is not necessary that the duty neglected should have arisen out of a contract between the patient and the doctor. However, the duty may arise by a statute or otherwise; and if it is neglected, resulting in an injury to any person, he will get a right to sue for damages. There cannot be a liability for negligence unless there is a breach of some duty. Hence, no case of actionable negligence will arise unless the 'duty to be careful' exists. Thus, the idea of negligence and duty are strictly correlative, and there is no such thing as negligence in the abstract; negligence is simply neglect of some care which the doctor is bound by law to exercise towards his patients.

Austin defines negligence thus: "In case of negligence, a party performs not an act to which he is obliged; he breaks a positive duty." Therefore, when the doctor neglects the use of ordinary care and skill towards his patient (to whom he owes a duty of observing such care and skill) which results in an injury to the patient, there is a case for 'actionable negligence'.

No case of actionable negligence will arise unless the 'duty to be careful' exists

Dr. Gopinath Shenoy, medico legal consultant and specialist in the defense of doctors in the Consumer Forums/Commissions answers your queries relating to legal aspects of medical practice.

Medical Negligence

'Medical Negligence' means lack of reasonable care, skill or willful negligence on part of a doctor in respect of acceptance of a patient, while taking history, while examining, while carrying out diagnosis or investigations, or even while treating either medically or surgically etc. which may cause or result in some kind of injury or damage to or death of the patient. Two basic propositions laid down in law regarding liability for negligence are: firstly, "Breach of Duty" to care and secondly, standard of care, i.e. the practitioner must bring to his task a reasonable degree of skill, knowledge and exercise a reasonable degree of care with caution (neither the very highest, nor a very low degree of care).

Essential Components of Medical Negligence

On basis of various judicial pronouncements essentials of 'Medical Negligence' as are discernible, in brief and in so far as it is relatable to the medical profession, are as under:

1. The Doctor must owe a duty of care to the patient;
2. The Doctor must have made a breach of that duty;
3. The patient must have suffered damages due to the said breach.

The Supreme Court in the case of *Minu B. Mehta vs. B.R. Nayar*[12] has held that the right to receive compensation can only be against a person who is bound to compensate due to his failure to perform a legal obligation. This judgment has laid the above proposition prior to enactment of the CP Act. The Supreme Court in the case of *Kaushnuma Begum vs. New India Assurance*,[13] while dealing with a case of defence of no fault liability under Motor Accident Claim, has held that Rule of strict liability enunciated in *Rylands vs. Fletcher* (1981-73) All E.R.Rep.1, can be followed, till a new and better principle is evolved or a different situation is created by legislation.

Sidaway vs. Bethlem Royal Hospital Governors, (1985) 1 ALL ER 643 (English case) [*Negligence and prevailing professional practice*]

(a) For establishing negligence in diagnosis or treatment on the part of a doctor, the true test is, whether he has been proved to be guilty of such failure, as no doctor of ordinary skill would be guilty of, if acting with ordinary care.
(b) The test of liability, in respect of a doctor's duty to warn his patient of risks inherent in the treatment recommended by him, is the same as the test applicable to diagnosis and

treatment, namely, that the doctor is required to act in accordance with a practice accepted at the time as proper, by a responsible body of medical opinion.

(c) Accordingly, a doctor charged with negligence can clear himself, if he shows that he acted in accordance with the prevailing professional practice.

(d) In the *Bolam case* the test was thus laid down. A doctor is not negligent, if he is acting in accordance with a practice accepted as proper by a responsible body of medical men skilled in that particular act, merely because there is a body of such opinion that takes a contrary view.

Negligence in Sterilization

Patient had undergone a sterilization operation in a Government hospital. The patient developed high fever and abnormal pain; and, though her condition deteriorated, no step was taken to ascertain the cause of her ailment. When the "patient's condition became serious, the doctors re-opened the abdomen. A mop (towel), (left inside the peritoneal cavity during the previous operation) was removed and the abdomen was closed, after draining out the collected pus. The patient ultimately died. The Supreme Court held that once death by negligence in a Government hospital is established, the State is liable to pay compensation.[14]

Foreign matter left in body after Operation

The doctor who operated upon the complainant for caesarian operation left something foreign inside the operated area. That being negligence in itself a compensation of Rs. 2 lakhs was awarded. The fact that no fee was taken for the operation and only the charges for the operation theatre and medicines were taken was held to be no defence. The complainant was a consumer because she paid for the services.[15]

Contaminated Blood Transfusion

In Shefali Bhargava vs. Indraprastha Apollo Hospital,[16] as a result of transfusion of contaminated blood, the patient got acute attack of

Hepatitis-C. There was no explanation as to why mother's blood which matched the patient was not used as a safer option.

It was held that as a result of the failure to take necessary care and caution in transfusing the blood, young life was seriously affected for which compensation of Rs. 10 lakhs was awarded towards the cost of medical treatment and Rs. 8 lakhs towards the cost of further treatment apart from Rs. 10,000 as costs.

Homeopathic Practitioner Prescribing Allopathy Medicine

A registered homeopath administered, to the patient suffering from guinea worm, 24 drops of straminium and a leaf of *dhatura*, without studying its effect; and the patient died of poisoning. This rash and negligent act of the doctor, in prescribing poisonous medicines without studying their probable effect, was of such a degree, as to amount to taking a hazard hereby injury was most likely to be occasioned.

The criminality lies, in running the risk of doing such an act with recklessness or indifference to the consequences. The homeopath doctor was held guilty under Section 304A of the Indian Penal Code (rash or negligent homicide).[17]

What is Medical Malpractice?

Medical malpractice occurs when a doctor or health care provider does not treat a medical condition properly and, as a result, causes a new or aggravated injury to the patient.

What types of Medical Malpractice are there?

Medical malpractice happens in a variety of situations, including but not limited to:

(a) Birth injury caused by failure to deliver a baby in a timely manner
(b) Delay or failure in diagnosing a disease or condition
(c) Surgical or anesthesia-related mishap during an operation
(d) Failure to gain the "informed consent" of the patient for an operation or surgical procedure, i.e., failing to disclose to the patient the risks associated with the procedure

(e) Failure to properly treat the disease process after making a correct diagnosis
(f) Misuse of prescription drugs or a medical device or implant

What is "Informed Consent?"

Physicians are required to inform their patients of the projected effectiveness of any proposed treatment, and the possibility of negative side effects or other adverse outcomes. Thus, before a doctor can perform a procedure, prescribe a drug, or take any significant action, he must get the "informed consent" of the patient.

Medical Malpractice: Failure to Diagnose

"One out of every five patients who die in the intensive care units of the nation's best hospitals has been misdiagnosed."

This conclusion was reached by a study of patient deaths between 1994 and 1996 at the prestigious Cleveland Clinic, and published in the *Journal Chest.* These findings, researchers said, closely mirror what goes on in ICUs across the country and have not changed dramatically since the study's conclusion. These medical providers are not necessarily guilty of medical malpractice because by definition, people admitted to ICUs are extremely ill and some of them have multiple medical problems. But if the medical providers reached the wrong conclusion because they failed to take an adequate medical history, perform the right tests or recognize the obvious symptoms of a particular illness, and their misdiagnosis is compounded by errors that would not be expected of any well-trained physician the their conduct may be considered malpractice.

A doctor may be liable for a misdiagnosis if:

(a) the patient is treated for a disease he does not have and the treatment causes injury,
(b) the patient expects treatment of one condition, but has obvious symptoms of another, and
(c) the patient receives medical advice that prevents treatment for a condition that later causes harm.

Concept of Reasonable Amount of Care

The professional ethics and Courts, both expect from the Doctor a reasonable amount of care, which any other doctor of reasonable skill would do or render under the situation. The concept of reasonable amount of care would differ in case of a specialist/expert and would be deemed to be the care, which any other expert/specialist on the subject would have rendered under the situation. If a patient goes to a general practitioner, he cannot expect the treatment, which a specialist is expected to render to the patient, even though condition of the patient is same. The expertise of treatment may differ from doctor to doctor, institution to institution, and patient to patient, but under given circumstances the law does not expect more than what any other doctor of normal skill would do.

Standard of Care

Lord Clyde has observed as "In the realm of diagnosis and treatment, there is ample scope for genuine difference of opinion, and one man clearly is not negligent, merely because his conclusion differs from that of other professional men, not because he has displayed less skill or knowledge than others would have shown. The true test for establishing negligence in diagnosis or treatment on the part of a doctor is, whether he has been proved to be guilty of such failure as no doctor of ordinary skill would be guilty of, if acting with ordinary care".[18]

Non-Providing of Anesthesia

(*Death due to repair of fracture of femur of leg, without anesthesia*)

Owing to an accident, the patient was suffering from fracture of the femur of his left leg. On screening, it was found that he had an overlapping fracture of the femur, which required pin-traction. A morphia injection was given to the patient. The doctor used manual traction with the help of three male attendants, at the time of putting the fractured leg in plaster. The kind of rough manipulation was calculated to cause conditions favourable for embolism or shock and proved fatal to the patient. The doctor described the cause of death as "fat embolism". The question for consideration was, whether the doctor was negligent. The Supreme Court held that the doctor was guilty of negligence and carelessness, because he did not make a thorough preliminary examination, before injecting morphia and he reduced the fracture, without taking elementary caution of giving an anesthetic to the patient.[19]

Law

The doctors owe a duty of care to their patients. Failure to show due care or skill in medical treatment, resulting in death, of the patient or injury or pain of, gives rise to a cause of action in negligence. Shelat, J., delivering the judgment of the Supreme Court of India, laid down the criteria for determination of the professional duty of a medical man, in the following words:

"A person, who holds himself out ready to give medical advice and treatment, impliedly undertakes that he is possessed of skill and knowledge for the purpose. Such a person, when consulted by a patient, owes him certain duties, viz. a duty of care in deciding whether to undertake the case, a duty of care in deciding what treatment to give, and a duty of care in the administration of that treatment. A breach of any of those duties gives a right of action for negligence to the patient. The practitioner must bring to his task a reasonable degree of skill and knowledge."

Res Ipsa Loquitur ('The Things Speak for Itself')

The doctrine of *res ipsa loquitur* means, that the accident speaks for itself or tells its own story. The normal rule is that it is for the plaintiff to prove negligence, but, in some cases, considerable hardship is caused to the plaintiff, as the true cause of the accident is not known to him, but is solely within the knowledge of the defendant who caused it. The plaintiff can prove the accident but cannot prove how it happened (so as) to establish negligence on the part of the defendant. This hardship is sought to be avoided, by invoking the principle of *res ipsa loquitur*, where the thing is shown to be under the management of the defendant or his servants, and the accident is such, as, in the ordinary course of things, does not happen if those who have the management use proper care, then it affords reasonable evidence, in the absence of an explanation by the defendant, that the accident arose from want of care.

Shyam Sunder *vs.* State of Rajasthan[20]

[*Scott vs. London & Catherine Docks*, (1965) 3 H&C 596 quoted in '*Shyam Sunder vs. State of Rajasthan*', AIR 1974 SC 896].

For the applicability of the principle of *res ipsa loquitur*, three essential conditions are normally considered to be essential:

(a) The opposite party must have been in control of things;
(b) Common knowledge/accepted norms suggesting that the injury/damage/loss, in itself cannot occur without negligence; and
(c) The cause of incident/injury must be unknown or unascertainable.

Some of the common instances, where this principle can be invoked, are operation on a wrong patient or a wrong part of the body, transfusion of improper blood, leaving some foreign material in the body, performing an abortion or any other operation or surgery which is prohibited in law, etc.

Volenti Non Fit Injuria

The maxim '*Volenti non fit injuria*', which is duly recognised and established principle and can be of great help to the doctors. It is a well-settled proposition of law that the person must bear loss arising from acts, which he assented. But by this principle, if the complainant has given his express consent, and prior thereto he was made aware or he was aware of the consequences, then he cannot sue the doctor for damage or loss, which may have occurred due to actions, which have been consented by the complainant.

Contributory Negligence

Where the negligence has either occasioned due to some factor which can be said to be contributory to happening of the event on part of the complainant or patient. This principle of contributory negligence takes care of such situations, where the event, which is complained of would not have taken place, if the complainant also would have been vigilant enough. Some instances of contributory negligence are non-communication of complete background/history of the patient, at the time of diagnosis and treatment, not providing reasonable amount of co-operation in taking precautions, in taking medications especially in prescribed quantity and on desired time, etc.

Medical Negligence in Emergency and Other Situations

Medical Council of India has clear guidelines on doctors' duty to a patient in emergency on humanitarian grounds. The Hon'ble Supreme Court had on different occasions, passed various directions that even the private doctors are bound to provide first aid to all patients coming to them, in case of emergency, irrespective of the fact that the said patient is in a position to pay or not and cannot refuse to provide first aid to any one. Attention is drawn here to famous judgment of the Supreme Court in *R.N. Katara's PIL* regarding first aid and initial life saving medical aid by medical men to trauma patients. The Courts at times, while dealing with situations of strikes in government hospitals, have also invoked the dictum of Article 21 of the Constitution, which mandates for right to life.

Conclusions

Neuro-physician's failure to attend to the patient in critical condition or give any instruction to the hospital staff for treatment of the patient which ultimately resulted in patient's death—Negligence.[21]

Improper Investigation of Disease—Deficiency in Service

Poonam Verma vs. Aswin Patel.[22]

A homeopathic practitioner treated the patient for eight days, by administering strong antibiotics initially for the treatment of viral fever and subsequently for typhoid fever, without confirming the diagnosis by any pathological test. The doctor also prescribed intramuscular injection of sodium compound, to relieve the patient of pain, without ascertaining the cause for the pain. The Supreme Court of India held the doctor guilty of negligence, in giving medicine without confirming his diagnosis by pathological tests.

The judgment stresses the need for proper investigation before prescribing a specific treatment—particularly, antibiotics.

Revealing of HIV Positive by Hospital—No Deficiency in Service[23]

Mr. X vs. Z (Hospital)(1999) CTJ 1 (SC)

Petitioner Dr. T had occasion to offer his blood for a friend undergoing treatment in the respondent, Apollo Hospital at Madras. Petitioner was found to be HIV positive. Doctors of the respondent Apollo Hospital disclosed this fact to a girl who was the petitioner's fiancée. As a result, the fiancée called off the proposed marriage. The petitioner then moved the court for damages against the hospital, for breach of the duty of professional secrecy.

The Supreme Court held that in the circumstances of the case, the hospital had not committed any illegality. The fiancée had a right to health, as a part of the right to life guaranteed by Article 21 of the Constitution; and, in order to protect that right, the disclosure was necessary. Fiancée's right to health overrode the petitioner's right to the maintenance of secrecy.

Moreover (according to the Supreme Court), if the (proposed) marriage had been solemnized in this case, then the petitioner (prospective husband) would have been guilty of the offence of knowingly spreading a malignant disease. Hence, the petitioner could not succeed.

How far should Doctors be held liable?

CCC & IMA Hold Joint Workshop to Improve Patient-Doctor Relationship

With a view to make the health services in India affordable and accessible for the poor while at the same time protect the interest of the patients and doctors, the Indian Medical Association (IMA) and Consumer Coordination Council (CCC) held a joint workshop in Trivandrum from the 10th-12th of September, 2004. The workshop had eminent speakers from both the medical fraternity as well as the Consumer Organizations including speakers from World Health Organizations, the Insurance Sector and the Central and State Government.

Some of the presentations during the 3rd day workshop are included herein,

- Consumer Protection Act and The Medical Services by Shri Bejon Misra, Chairman, CCC.
- Doctor-Patient Relationship in the Current Context by Dr. N.K. Grover, Past National President, IMA.
- Identifying Causes for Existing Gaps in Patient Doctor Relationship and Initiation of Steps for Building up of

Healthy Relationship between them by Joint Efforts by IMA and CCC.

- Presentation by Ms. Shubhra Singh, Department of Family Welfare, Government of India.
- *Client Provider Relationship*—West Bengal Experience by Dr. Rajat Das, Kolkata, West Bengal.
- During the workshop, there were intense discussions highlighting the problems faced by the patients and doctors.
- *Identifying Causes for Existing Gaps in Patient-Doctor Relationship* and initiation of steps for building up of healthy relationship between them with the joint efforts by IMA and CCC.
- Developing a code of conduct for Medical Practitioners and Patients in the context of the existing legislations.
- Identifying measures for providing Quality Medical Services at affordable costs.

"Actio Personalis Moritur cum Persona"

Means that *the personal right of action dies with the person.* In other words, death destroys the right of action. The right to sue will be extinguished.

Winfield: Law of Torts, 8th Edition

At Page 740, the following passage occurs: "in case of a lawful surgical operation in general negatives the liability. But in a case where actionable negligence is committed by the doctor which amounts to a personal wrong done by him, he may be liable for damages. But his death extinguished his liability in tort and the right to sue also gets extinguished".

In *Jayaprakash vs. State of Andhra Pradesh*[24] the Supreme Court held "The death of the doctor extinguished his liability for damages and the suit against him stood abated".

Conclusion

India's consumer courts, which are located in districts across the country, are intended to offer a speedy alternative to civil courts, where cases often drag on for many years. The Indian Medical Association had campaigned against the inclusion of medical services under the Consumer Protection Act on the grounds that medical services could not be equated with consumer transactions involving ordinary products and services.

"The patient-doctor relationship is complex and not the same as that of a producer and consumer," said Dr. Bharat Chharparwal, president of the Indian Medical Association. Dr. Jagdish Sobti, honorary secretary of the association, said: "Feelings of mutual distrust might creep in." Doctors have also expressed concern that the promise of quick verdicts from consumer courts might prompt some consumers to file false complaints.

An estimated 8,000 cases against doctors are pending in consumer courts. The charges range from unnecessary surgical operations or inappropriate treatment to medical negligence leading to disabilities or deaths of patients. Consumer groups say that, since many doctors treat the medical profession as just a business, medical services should be covered under the Consumer Protection Act.

The Supreme Court's judgment classifies doctors and hospitals into three categories—those who charge all patients, those who charge some patients and offer free services to others, and those where medical services are rendered free to all patients. The court said that services rendered by the first two categories will fall within the ambit of consumer courts.

Some doctors have hinted that patients could incur higher expenses for medical treatment as a result of the court ruling. "More doctors are likely to practice defensive medicine and order detailed investigations so as to be absolutely sure of the illness before prescribing treatment," said Dr. Chharparwal.

Members of the Indian Medical Association are to seek additional safeguards to prevent doctors from being harassed under the Act. There is a provision for a 10000 rupee (pounds sterling 200) penalty for consumers filing false or frivolous complaints—Ganapati Mudur, science writer, New Delhi. Therefore, doctors must realize that while courts are very considerate when dealing with negligence cases against doctors, but when found guilty the due award of compensation is likely to be given in favour of aggrieved patient/his legal heirs. It is worth noting that under civil law government hospitals are equally liable for negligence in treatment. It is hoped that proper lessons will be learnt from these judgments as they become "bench-mark" for future cases with similar situations.

NOTES

1. B.S.Sindhu *vs.* Secretary, Central Government Post and Telegraph Department (1991) 2 CPJ 90 Har.
2. Spring Meadows Hospital *vs.* Harjot Ahluwalia, AIR 1998 SC 1801; (1998) 1 CPR 1; (1998) 4 SCC 39 (SC).
3. Rajaram S.Parale *vs.* Dr. Kalpana Desai, (1998) 3 CPR 398 (Bombay).
4. AIR 1996 SC 550; (1995) 6 3CC 651 3 CPR 412 (SC).
5. Nilabati Behera *vs.* State of Orissa, AIR 1993 SC 1960.
6. (1997) CPJ 481 (HC of AP)].
7. II 1992 CPJ 449.
8. II (1994) CPJ 523.
9. I (1992) CCPJ 302 (April 92 Appeals No. 48 & 94 of 1991).
10. Consumer Education and Research Society and another *vs.* Dr. Rati Lal B. Patel and others III (1992) CPJ 25 dated 3rd May, 1993 in OP No. 92/93.
11. [Poonam Verma *vs.* Ashwin Patel and Others. (Supreme Court Civil Appeal No. 8856 of 1994. Decided on 10th May, 1996].
12. 1977 (2) SCC 441.
13. 2001 (2) SCC 9.
14. Achutrao Haribhau Khodwa *vs.* State of Maharashtra, (1996) 2 SCC 634.
15. Rohini Pritam Kabadi *vs.* R.T. Kulkarni (Dr.), (1996) 3 CPJ 441 Kant.
16. I (2003) CPJ 216 (NC).
17. Juggankhan *vs.* State of M.P., AIR 1965 SC 831; (1965) 2 SCJ 119 (Criminal Case).
18. Hunter *vs.* Hanley (W5) Scotish Law Times 213, (1955) Scotish c&3es 200.
19. Laxman Balkrishna Joshi (Dr.) *vs.* Dr. Trimbak Bapu Godbole, AIR 1969 SC 128 must exercise a reasonable degree of care.
20. AIR 1974 SC 896; (1974)1 SCC 690; (1974) ACJ 296; (1974) 2 SCJ 317.
21. Murlidhar Eknath Masane *vs.* Sushrusha citizen Co-op Hospital Ltd (1995) I CPR 606 (Mah).
22. AIR 1996 SC 2111; (1996) 4 SCC 662; (1996) 3 CPR 205; (1996) 4 CTJ 465 (SC) (CP).
23. Tokughayepthoma *vs.* Apollo Hospital Enterprises, (1998) 3M CPJ 12 (SC); (1999) CCJ 467 (SC).
24. AIR 1977 AP 20 at p. 22.

PART IV

Services in Transport

Chapter 9

Indian Railways and Consumer Welfare

D.S. MAKKALANBAN

Introduction

The Indian Railways started its journey in 1858 and now it has grown into one of the biggest service providers to the people. Indian Railways stand first in terms of number of employees and the largest of railway networks in the world. Railways have become a life-line of Indian transport system. Indian Railways have been divided into 9 major divisions (zones) previously and now it has been further extended to 16 divisions.

Consumer's Grievances

Traffic is heaviest on the tracks of Indian Railways. Indian Railways transports both men and materials. While the commuters pay for goods and services, the former is visible one and the latter is invisible one with also being everyone's moral responsibility and professional obligation. Yet trains are invariably late; long distance trains are found to be without water, and electricity due to paucity of maintenance, travelling ticket examiners do not bother to check unauthorized entry of passengers in reserved compartments, passengers given reserved accommodations by the train conductors are arbitrarily fined by the anti-fraud squad sometimes and often bogies are not attached resulting in inconvenience to passengers holding tickets (they have to finally travel in unreserved compartments defeating the very purpose of reservation). The reservation of seats by local vendors in unreserved

(General) compartments is of big headache for the travellers, as they often get in quarrel with travellers. They occupy the seat and leave it for passengers who give some money to them (a form of bribe). The railway authorities are least bothered to care for such illegal happenings in railway stations.

Over crowding, in general compartment is the big nuisance to the passengers. The quality of food is very poor and also not hygienic served by catering authorities. Moreover, the cost of food items in trains are not fair, passengers use to give exorbitant rates from buying even a mineral water. Ticketless travellers occupying the seats of reserved passengers, committing nuisance, and they are always being a hindrance to the people. Though the Travelling Ticket Examiner (TTE) is available then and there, but he never bothers of such incidents. Heavy pricing of food beverages are not affordable to each and everyone who travel in the train. Apart from which the cleanliness of railway stations and latrine facilities invites much criticism for not being properly maintained.

And to add to the trauma of commuters, rail accidents have become frequent, a sign of authorities not concerned with the safety and well being of passengers. Unfortunately, all of us grumble, but hardly anyone comes forward to book the railways for its glaring (sometimes fatal) errors. At the same time the passengers use to experience certain unexpected/unwanted scenes during their journey. However the hospitality in the railway sector especially in railway is pitiable. Lack of medical facilities, delayed departure and arrivals, theft, looting arsenal are some of the day-to-day scenes experiences by the passengers. Now-a-days, it is also much overcrowded in the reservation hall and one needs to spend atleast 15 to 30 minutes to book a ticket. Even to avail the ticket to travel in general compartment one needs to spend atleast the same amount of time that highly kills traveller's time and energy. Though we do have consumer redressal forum to redress the grievances, they are not as active in redressing the grievances of the passengers. Moreover, only a minimal number of people are approaching the forums and get their grievances addressed.

Compensation

The Consumer Protection Act, 1986 is an Act to provide for better protection of the interests of consumers and for that purpose to make provision for the establishment of consumer councils and other authorities for the settlement of consumer's disputes and for matters connected therewith.

As per the Railways Act of 1989, all the passengers, platform ticket holders are insured against train accidents, death and injury on account of untoward incidents. Untoward incidents include commission of a terrorist attack, violent-attacks, robbery, dacoit, rioting, arson etc.

Remedy

Before talking about the legal rights regarding deficiency in the service of the railways and the remedy available under the Consumer Protection Act, it will be necessary first to deal with the Railway Claims Tribunal Act and other similar legislations. These prohibit the filing of certain types of complaints which are heard several years later and dismissed because the consumer forum does not have jurisdiction to entertain such complaints. The Railway Claims Tribunal Act, 1987, confers exclusive jurisdiction on the Railway Claims Tribunal. In case the claimant is not satisfied with the relief provided by the Railways, he can seek legal remedy through the Railway Claims Tribunal, which has been set up under the Railway Claims Tribunal Act, 1987 which came into force from 8th November 1989. The Tribunal has 21 benches at 18 major cities in the country to deal with the following types of cases:

(a) Claims or compensation for loss, destruction, damage, deterioration or non-delivery of animals or goods;
(b) Claims for refund for fares or for refund of any freight paid in respect of animals or goods; and
(c) Claims in respect of railway accidents.

The Consumer Protection Act is in addition to and not interrogation of any other law, which may be in force. In the above three types of claims, the legislature has ousted the jurisdiction of all courts and granted exclusive jurisdiction only to the Railway Claims Tribunal. The Consumer Protection Act cannot override the bar under the Railway Claims Tribunal Act, and hence complaints regarding such cases cannot be filed before consumer forums. Similarly, compensation cannot be sought for delay in delivery of goods because of the Coaching Tariff Rule states that the Railways do not guarantee dispatch of articles or animals by any particular train or deliver within a stipulate time period. Unfortunately, while talking about competition, liberalization and globalization, the Centre continues with outdated rules that promote inefficiency by providing complete protection and lack of accountability. Thus, the essence of '*service*' in Consumer Protection Act is at stake, that states "service" means service of any description which is made available to potential users and includes the provision of facilities in connection with banking, financing, insurance, transport, processing, supply of electrical or other energy, board or lodging or both [housing construction], entertainment, amusement, or the purveying of news or other information, but does not include the rendering of any service free of charge or under a contract of personal service.[1]

All this, is to be admitted is grim. But there are aspects where consumer courts have won justice for those who have suffered due to negligence of the Railways. Some of the landmark judgments on these issues are:

(a) Mrs. Kabita Hansaria was travelling by Tinsukhia Mail from Delhi to Guwahati. While moving from one coach to another through the corridor/vestibule, she fell down and died. A case was filed in the consumer court. In appeal, the National Commission distinguished between a "railway accident" and an "accidental death", and held that since there had been an accidental death but no railway accident, the consumer forum had jurisdiction to entertain the complaint. The legal heirs were awarded a compensation of Rs. 2,25,000.

(b) Manoj Pathak and his parents had confirmed reservation to travel from Bombay Central to Ahmedabad by the Gujarat Express. Unauthorized persons boarded the train enroute. The complainant attempted to seek help of the ticket checker but was unsuccessful. When he attempted to resist the illegal entry of persons in a reserved compartment, he was beaten up and his vertebral column suffered a fracture resulting in a 10 per cent permanent bodily disability. The National Commission ultimately held that the compensation of Rs. 56,000 awarded by the lower forums was justified and dismissed the revision petition filed by the Railways with costs of Rs. 1,000 payable to the complainant.

(c) Dr. Pramod Kumar Agarwal had five confirmed tickets to travel from Allahabad to Howrah by Kalka Mail. As the train was late, Dr. Kumar approached the conductor of Chambal Express who made the necessary endorsement on the ticket, permitting him to travel by this train. The anti-fraud squad refused to recognize the endorsement and fined Dr. Agarwal for ticketless travel. The National Commission, in revision, held that the complainant was entitled to a refund of the fare and penalty which had wrongly been charged.

(d) One of the passengers Mrs. Reena[2] (name changed), who was travelling with jewellery from a marriage she had attended, lost the entire lot—necklaces, bangles and several precious gems. Alleging "deficiency of service" in opposition to the Railways, she filed a consumer complaint with the concerned State Commission looking for compensation. [For claims of exceeding than Rs. 20 lakhs, the grievance must be filed directly before the State Commission.] The State Commission went into the particulars of the complaint and found the case in her favour. The Railway Administration was accordingly directed to pay her compensation. Unhappy with this order, the Railways filed an petition before the National Commission.

Jurisdiction Challenged

Here, the Railway Administration advanced an argument challenging the jurisdiction of the Consumer Dispute Redressal Fora in taking up complaints of this type. They contended that the correct Forum was the Railway Claims Tribunal. They also argued that the entry of unauthorized persons into the compartment and loss of luggage and harm caused by such persons had nothing to do with the legal responsibility of the Railway Administration. Eventually, the National Commission acknowledged this argument that there was no 'deficiency' in their service.

This case subsequently went before the Supreme Court of India, where arguments were advanced for both parties. The Supreme Court went through all the related facts of the complaint and disagreed with the decision of the National Commission. Specifically on the issue of jurisdiction, the Supreme Court observed, "even otherwise, under Section 3 of the Consumer Protection Act, the complaint might be entertained by the State Commission". The Court went on to turn over the National Commission order and restored to life the State Commission's order for compensation.

The important issue here is Section 3 of the Consumer Protection Act, which reads "The provisions of this Act shall be in addition to and not in derogation of the provisions of any other law for the time being in force."[3] Cutting through the legalese, this means that the Consumer Protection Act and the remedies it provides can be used by consumers in addition to any additional remedies that may exist under any other law. Therefore, in the instant case, Mrs. Reena could file for reparation under the Consumer Protection Act irrespective of her rights to claim such compensation under the Railway Claims Tribunal Act.

Conclusion

The Section 3 of the Consumer Protection Act is measured by many scholars of consumer law as being the strongest and most effective section. Further, since Consumer Dispute Redressal Fora are established in every single district in this country under this law, Section 3 allows millions of consumers to access justice at their own districts—an accomplishment unmatched by any alike law. It is significant to concede that effort was made by a part of sellers and service providers to pull down Section 3 a few years ago, but the Indian Parliament did not allow this to happen.

Consumers around the country must recognize that the Consumer Protection Act is not just a step in the right direction, but a remarkably large step. But a law can remain just a piece of paper, if citizens do not make it work. And therefore, it is crucial that all of us emphasize our rights, and use the extraordinary provisions of this law.

Consumer Service/ Railways related Cases are handled by:

The Passengers and Traffic Relief Association
(*Dial: 2043168—3.00 p.m. to 6.00 p.m.*)
Anand Bhavani (Siddhartha College Building)
IIIrd Floor, Above Great Western Stores,
DN Road, Fort, Mumbai—400 001, India.

It is one of the oldest voluntary consumer organizations in the country, having been established in 1915. It takes up complaints against the railways and attempts to sort out the matter amicably. The issues taken up are both of general nature as well as specific complaints.

NOTES

1. The Consumer Protection Act, 1986 [Act No. 68 of 1986] [As amended by Act No. 62 of 2002].
2. Bharath Jairaj, CAG, e-mail: cag.helpdesk@gmail.com.
3. Consumer Protection Act, 1986.

REFERENCES

Arora, Renu (2005). *Consumer Grievances Redressal,* New Delhi: Manak.

Consumer Protection Regulations, 2005.

Himachalam, D. (1998). *Consumer Protection and the Law,* New Delhi: Deep and Deep.

The Consumer Protection Act, 1986, (68 of 1986) 24th December.

The Consumer Protection Rules, 1987.

www.consumeronline.org.

PART V

Services in Insurance

Chapter 10

Consumer Rights in Insurance Industry

T.G. ETHIRAJULU

Regarding the insurance industry the consumer (policy-holder) should know the entire details of the areas how he/she should receive various claims. In the year 2002, a body called Insurance Regulatory and Development Authority (IRDA) was instituted in protecting the policy holder's interest.

The areas the consumer should take note regarding life insurance are:

(a) Receipt of the policy bond in original.
(b) Survival benefit claim.
(c) Maturity claims
(d) Death claims.
(e) Assignment and Nomination.

Receipt of Policy Bond

All policy holders should be aware that he should receive the original policy bond in time. If he had not received, he/she should contact the concerned Branch Office immediately.

Survival Benefit Claim

In the money back policies, the policy-holder is entitled to receive some percentage of the sum assured at regular intervals. If he/she had not received the money on time they can approach the "Claims Department" of the concerned Branch Office.

Maturity Claims

All policy-holders are eligible to receive the maturity claim money after the end of the contract. At present, LIC of India dispatches the relevant vouchers 90 days in advance to the policy-holder—thereby the maturity claim can be prepared well in advance and settled in time. The policy-holder should submit the voucher and the original document to the insurance company to get his maturity.

Death Claims

The nominees of the policy-holder are eligible to receive the death claim. This is an important area both for the Insurance Company as well as the policy-holder. If the death is a natural death the following papers should be submitted to the insurance company by the claimant:

(a) Letter of death intimation.
(b) Filled in claim forms properly attested and witnessed.
(c) Original death certificate.
(d) Discharge voucher signed by the nominee.
(e) Original policy bond.
(f) Hospital certificate (only for hospitalized cases).

If the death is by accident then the claimant should submit:

(a) FIR copy.
(b) Police inquest report.
(c) All other above mentioned forms.

If the death claim is before the expiry of three years from the date of commencement of the policy then it is termed as "Early claim" If the death is by early claims the claims will be settled only on proper investigation by the Insurance Officers.

Nomination

The proposer has to nominate at the time of submitting the proposal (or) he can appoint a nominee by writing a letter to the insurance company. Minors also can be appointed as nominee but there should be an appointee to receive the death claim on behalf of the nominee.

Assignment

Regarding Assignment, it can be done in two ways:

(a) By endorsement on the back of the policy.
(b) By way of deed after paying necessary stamp duty.

Assignment will come into effect only when it is registered with Insurance Company and on Assignment, the nomination will be automatically cancelled. Hence, fresh nomination should be made after re-assignment of the policy.

The areas the consumers should take note in General Insurance are:

(a) Motor Claim.
(b) Mediclaim.
(c) Fire Insurance Claims.

Motor Claim

(a) Claim should be intimated immediately.
(b) Filling claim form and getting estimate from the repairer.
(c) After the inspection is over the repair can be done and on production of the bills the amount will be refunded to the tune of the amount sanctioned by the surveyor.

Mediclaim

(a) Claim intimation immediately (or) with in 7 days.
(b) If it is cashless option, sanction of cashless option from the TPA.
(c) If it is re-imbursement, productions of all the bills along with claim form duly filled.

Fire Insurance Claim

(a) Claim to be intimated immediately.
(b) Police reports.
(c) Stock report.

(d) After the inspection of the surveyor the claim is paid.

The following Department/Officers to be contacted for redressal of are grievance by the consumer/policy-holder before going to any court of law for their problems.

Stages

1. Administrative Officers	— In the Branch Offices.
2. Branch Managers	— Available on every Monday of the week in Branches to redress the grievances. (No appointment is required).
3. Marketing Manager	— In the Divisional Offices. (Appointment is necessary)
4. Manager (Claims)	— In the Divisional Offices (Redressal of all claims).
5. Senior Divisional Manager	— In the Divisional Offices (Appointment is a must)
6. Customer Relations Manager	— Available in Divisional Office.
7. Regional Manager	— In the Regional Office (LIC Building Mount Road)
8. Zonal Manager	— In the Zonal Office (LIC Building Mount Road)
9. Ombudsman	— Office of the Insurance Ombudsman Fathima Akthtar Court, 4th Floor New No. 453, Old No. 312 Annasalai, Teynampet Chennai-600018. Phone Number—24333668.

Chapter 11

Consumer Rights in Service Sector: A Case Study of Deficiency in Service in the Insurance Sector

S. S. PANKAJAM

"Consumer Rights in Service Sector", is a subject which has acquired special significance in modern times, by reason of predominance of deficiency in services in all sectors.

Who is a Consumer?

A consumer may be regarded as any one who consumes goods or services at the end of the chain of production. It means any person who buys any goods for a consideration or hires any services for a consideration which has been paid or partly paid and partly promised, or under any system of deferred payment and includes any beneficiary of such services other than the person who hires the services for consideration paid or promised, or partly paid and partly promised or under any system of deferred payment, when such services are availed of with approval of the first mentioned person. The term hire covers the field of service covering both the private and public sectors.

The concepts of Mr. Chrismoore that customers are the most important people in business deals and without them there can be no sales or services, does no longer stand the test in these days. The consumers in India form one of the most exploited classes of people of this country. They are disorganized and ignorant and have become the victims of dishonesty.

As the consumers were disorganized, they could not make their grievances audible to the persons in the helm of affairs, and they continued to suffer worst exploitation. A large percentage of the consumers in India live below the poverty line. They are mostly illiterate. They have little information and knowledge about their rights. On the other hand, services rendered to the consumers for consideration frequently suffer from fault, imperfection, short coming and inadequacy in quality, nature and manner of performance. In fact trade monopoly and market complexities have assured such magnitude that in their whirlwind the consumer as a class is feeling worst suffocation. The Government in our country is the largest supplier of services enjoying monopoly trade in most of them. In the supply of essential public services such as electricity, transport, communication and banking, all the available evidence points out a woeful lack of concern for the consumer. This gives an idea about the condition of the consumers in India, the extent of their helplessness and ignorance and this deplorable state of the consumers attracted the attention of the Central Government, who enacted "The Consumer Protection Act in 1986".

The 20-point programme is a renewed commitment of the Government to its relentless war on poverty and generally to improve the quality of life across the land. In fulfilment of the then Prime Minister, Mr. Rajiv Gandhi's Independence Day Assurance, a restructured 20-point programme was unveiled in Parliament on August 20, 1986.

In furtherance of the 20-point programme of the Central Government, Parliament enacted the law which received the assent of the President on 24.12.1986. The Act is a milestone in the history of socio-economic legislation in India. The Laws on this subject as prevalent in the United Kingdom, United States of America, Australia, and New Zealand were closely studied and considered before drafting the bill.

The Constitution of India in its preamble and also in the Directive Principles of State Policy under Article 38(1) has professed to promote the welfare of the people by securing and protecting as effectively, as it may, a social order permeated justice social, economic and political.

This Consumer Protection Act of 1986 is an important progressive and comprehensive piece of welfare legislation which seeks to achieve social and economic justice by protecting the interest of the consumers and for that purpose by making provisions for the establishment of consumer councils and other authorities for the settlement of consumer's disputes and for matters connected therewith. The Act is a sincere attempt to ameliorate the condition of the consumers in the society.

The Insurance and Service Sector

The Insurance Act, 1938 (Act No.4 of 1938) (26th February 1938):

An Act to consolidate and amend the law relating to the business of insurance.

The Indian Insurance Market has waited for more than five years for liberalization. Liberalization had opened the doors for many new companies into the Insurance Sector. As it is widely known, the Government in April 1993 set up a Committee on Insurance Sector Reforms popularly known as the Malhotra Committee.

"The R.N. Malhotra Committee" recommended sweeping reforms in the Insurance Sector in its report submitted to the then Finance Minister Dr. Manmohan Singh on January 7, 1994. The Committee, set-up under the Chairmanship of Mr. R.N. Malhotra, former Governor of Reserve Bank of India, recommended entry of the private sector in both life and general insurance business.

Highlights of the Malhotra Committee Report are:

(a) Permit private sector in insurance industry but with minimum paid up capital of Rs. 100 crores.
(b) Foreign companies, if permitted in insurance industry, should float Indian companies and preferably joint ventures with Indian partners.
(c) Controller of Insurance should be restored its full functions under the Insurance Act.

Following its recommendations in January 1994, the Government, in principle accepted the entry of private players in this sector. In addition to Indian companies, a number of international companies have evinced strong interest in entering the Indian Insurance Sector, both life and non-life or General Insurance. As a result, most of these new entrants are joint ventures with foreign concerns.

The Malhotra Committee, while recommending the opening up on the insurance industry to private players, rightly also recommended that the industry should be regulated in a proper manner. As a follow up of this recommendation an interim Insurance Regulatory Authority (IRA) was set up in 1996.

The Government has taken the initiative required to open up this long-delayed sector. The Lok Sabha passed the Insurance Regulatory and Development Authority (IRDA) Bill on December 2, 1999. Following this, the Rajya Sabha passed the Bill on December 7, 1999. The Bill became an Act after obtaining Presidential assent. The Insurance Act has given statutory status to IRDA. Simultaneously, the monopoly status of Government owned insurance companies has been reversed.

The Insurace industry as on 1.4.2000 comprised mainly two players

1. *Life Insurers*: Life Insurance Corporation of India (LIC).
2. *General Insurers*: General Insurance Corporation of India (GIC) (with effect from December 2000, a National Reinsurer).

GIC had four subsidiary companies, namely (with effect from December 2000) these subsidiaries have been de-linked from the parent company and made as independent insurance companies.

(a) The Oriental Insurance Company Limited.
(b) The New India Assurance Company Limited.
(c) National Insurance Company Limited.
(d) United India Insurance Company Limited.

Insurance Industry in the year 2000-2001 had 16 new entrants, namely

Life Insurers

(i) HDFC Standard Life Insurance Company Limited. (Date of Registration 23.10.2000)
(ii) Max New York Life Insurance Company Limited. (Date of Registration 15.11.2000)
(iii) ICICI Prudential Life Insurance Company Limited. (Date of Registration 24.11.2000)
(iv) Kotak Mahindra Old Mutual Life Insurance Limited. (Date of Registration 10.01.2001)
(v) Birla Sun Life Insurance Company Limited. (Date of Registration 31.01.2001)

(vi) Tata AIG Life Insurance Company Limited.
(Date of Registration 12.02.2001)
(vii) SBI Life Insurance Company Limited.
(Date of Registration 30.03.2001)
(viii) ING Vysya Life Insurance Company Private Limited.
(Date of Registration 02.08.2001)
(ix) Bajaj Allianz Life Insurance Company Limited.
(Date of Registration 03.08.2001)
(x) Metlife India Insurance Company Private Limited.
(Date of Registration 06.08.2001)

General Insurers

(xi) Royal Sundaram Alliance Insurance Company Limited.
(Date of Registration 23.10.2000)
(xii) Reliance General Insurance Company Limited.
(Date of Registration 23.10.2000)
(xiii) IFFCO Tokio General Insurance Company Limited.
(Date of Registration 04.12.2000)
(xiv) Tata AIG General Insurance Company Limited.
(Date of Registration 22.01.2001)
(xv) Bajaj Allianz General Insurance Company Limited.
(Date of Registration 02.05.2001)
(xvi) ICICI Lombard General Insurance Company Limited.
(Date of Registration 03.08.2001)

In the Year: 2001-2002 (From 1st January 2001 to December 2002)

Insurance Industry in this year, so far has 5 new entrants; namely

Life Insurers

(i) AMP Sanmar Life Insurance Company Limited.
(Date of Registration 03.01.2002)
(ii) Aviva Life Insurance Company Indian-Private Limited.
(Date of Registration 14.05.2002)

General Insurers

(iii) Cholamandalam General Insurance Company Limited.
(Date of Registration 15.07.2002)

(iv) Export Credit Guarantee Corporation Limited. (Date of Registration 27.08.2002)

(v) HDFC-Chubb General Insurance Company Limited. (Date of Registration 27.08.2002)

In the Year: 2003-2004

Insurance Industry in this year, so far has 1 new entrant; namely—

Life Insurers

(1) Sahara Indian Insurance Company Limited. (Date of Registration 06.02.2004)

In the Year: 2004-2005

Insurance Industry in this year, so far has 1 new entrant; namely—

Life Insurers

(1) Shriram Life Insurance Company Limited (Date of Registration 17.11.2005)

Ironically, with the increase in the number of competitors, instead of an increase or improvement in the quality of service there has been a deterioration and deficiency in their services.

A very apt case can be presented as an evidence of compromise in the quality of service:

BEFORE THE DISTRICT CONSUMER DISPUTES REDRESSAL FORUM

Mylapore, Chennai (South)
C.O.P. No. 463 of 2004

S.S. Pankajam .... Complainant

vs.

SBI Life Insurance Co. Ltd., Mumbai ... Ist Opposite Party

Sundaram Finance Limited (Deposits Department), Chennai-2.
[Corporate Agency (C.A. No.20493)
For SBI Life Insurance] ....2nd Opposite Party.

GIST OF THE CASE

This is a complaint filed before the District Consumer Disputes Redressal forum (South) at Mylapore, Chennai-600004.

The Complainant Mrs. S.S. Pankajam M.A., M.Phil, residing at Chennai.

The 1st Opposite Party is carrying on its business under the name and style of SBI Life Insurance Company and the same is a Limited Company having their Head Office at Mumabi. SBI Life Insurance Company Ltd. (SBI Life) is a joint venture of State Bank of India and Cardif S.A. of France. SBI is the largest Bank in India and Cardif S.A. is a leading Insurance Company in France operating in 25 countries. Cardif is a wholly owned subsidiary of BNP Paribas, one of the top 5 banks in the world.

The 2nd Opposite Party is the Corporate Agency of the 1st Opposite Party and their Corporate Agency number is 20493 and having their office at Pattulos Road, Chennai-600002.

The 1st Opposite Party made elaborate publications with regard to their various schemes in the Insurance Company. The Complainant on knowing the benefits of "SBI—Life Scholar Policy" approached the 2nd Opposite Party for availing it for her daughter as it is exclusively for kids. She made a proposal on 27.11.2002, and paid a sum of Rs. 3,317 to the 1st Opposite Party through the 2nd Opposite, Party which being the premium amount (Half yearly) for the said policy.

The 2nd Opposite Party accepted the Premium amount and assured that the Policy will be sent after complying with other formalities by the 1st Opposite Party. The Complainant states that as the said date was being the 2nd birthday of her daughter S. Yukthaa she had more sentimental value. The cheque having been issued by the Complainant was also honoured on 04.12.2002 in favour of 1st Opposite Party.

The Complainant submits that in the month of Feb. 2003 i.e., 22.02.2003 as per the instructions given through the 2nd Opposite Party by the 1st Opposite Party, the Complainant underwent medical test in Erlich Laboratory, Chennai-600014 and the Report was promised to be sent by the Laboratory confidentially to the 1st Opposite Party. Several months elapsed but no response had come either from the 1st Opposite Party or from the 2nd Opposite Party with regard to the issuance of the policy. The Complainant and her husband made frequent visits to the office of the 2nd Opposite Party with regard to the above and were informed that it was under process and the same would be received in a short span of time.

The Complainant started written communication with the Opposite Parties from 07.08.2003. The Complainant came to understand through the 2nd Opposite Party that a sum of Rs. 250 was to be paid as additional premium and to that effect, a communication was sent by 1st Opposite Party to the 2nd Opposite Party who had failed to inform/send the same to her.

After a lapse of 9 months, the complainant on knowing of the payment of Rs. 250 as additional premium went to the office of the 2nd opposite party and paid the said amount by means of DD. drawn on I.O.B. dated 07.08.2003. She was also further orally instructed by the 2nd opposite Party that she had to send the Echo Cardio Graphic Report. The same was also furnished along with the additional premium of Rs. 250 on 08.08.2003. After that, the Complainant was eagerly awaiting for the said policy. Finally, the Complainant was forced to send a letter at length to both the Opposite Parties by registered post on 25.02.2004. On 12.04.2004 the 1st Opposite Party replied the Complainant that they would not be able to consider the proposal for Life Insurance and instructed her to get assistance from the 2nd Opposite Party for further clarification. The said letter dated 12.04.2004 does not disclose the actual reason as to why the Insurance Company was not able to issue the policy after the receipt of premium amount.

The Complainant further states that after having taken a long time for considering the issuance of policy and all of a sudden return back of the premium amount alone is an act of negligence and deficiency in service. To the surprise of the Complainant, they failed to refund the additional premium amount for the reasons best known to them, after refunding the 1st premium. The Opposite Parties are guilty of lack of service and being reputed. Concern/s they must be vigilant and careful in issuing the policy after the receipt of premium amount. If they had not been satisfied on the proposal form, nothing prevented them in refunding the premium amount in time. The failure of the Opposite Parties can be taken as deficiency of service in rendering service to the Complainant.

In view of that the Complainant was put to mental agony, torture and strain as well as monetary loss. As the additional premium for Rs. 250 was not repaid by the 1st Opposite Party and also the 2nd Opposite Party, the Opposite parties could not simply reject the request of issuing the policy for the benefit of her daughter and other family members.

For the above "Deficiency of Service", the Complainant is entitled to claim the following reliefs:

Compensation for mental agony for not issuing the policy after the receipt of premium amount : Rs. 2,00,000

Cost of the proceedings : Rs. 5,000

Total Rs. 2,05,000

Apart from the above, a direction is seeked by the Complainant for issuing the policy from the date of paying the actual proposal i.e. 27.11.2002 with all benefits.

The Complainant states that she paid the premium amount on 27.11.2002 for the issuance of a policy under "SBI Life—Scholar" to the 1st Opposite Party and the premium amount was returned back without any reason after a period of 16 months and also keeping the additional premium with them and issued the communication to that effect by the 1st Opposite Party on 12.04.2004.

The cause of action arose at Chennai on 12.04.2004 on which date the Opposite Parties rejected the request of issuing the policy under the above said scheme and the Complainant also issued notice in her name for doing the same as her grievance is not redressed and her sincere attempts ended in vain, she was forced to knock the door of justice for redressing her grievance.

This case is now pending before the Honourable District Consumer Disputes Redressal-Forum (South), Mylapore, Chennai, for Directions /Orders.

The dates of the Proceedings of the Honourable Court are enlisted below:

30.04.2004	:	Complaint filed (Party in Person)
03.11.2004	:	Notice ordered
01.12.2004	:	Opposite 1 set exparte, Opposite 2 filed vak. for version
16.12.2004	:	For version of Opposite 2
17.12.2004	:	POL (Presiding Officer Leave)

03.01.2005	:	Version
13.01.2005	:	Amendment Petition
17.01.2005	:	MOLS: Amendment petition
20.01.2005	:	Amendment petition filed. MP: 102/05
02.02.2005	:	MP. Allowed for APC (Amended Petition Copy)
15.03.2005	:	Amendment carried out for APC, Opposite 2 filed version, Opposite 1 represented
11.04.2005	:	Amendment carried out for APC, Opposite 2 filed version, Opposite 1 represented
12.05.2005	:	No sitting for proof Affidavit
10.06.2005	:	P.A. (of Both)
12.07.2005	:	MP. 340/05 set aside filed, notice to respondent
21.07.2005	:	Notice to respondent Pvt.
17.08.2005	:	Notice
30.08.2005	:	AOS filed counter
08.09.2005	:	TE for counter
13.09.2005	:	Counter
13.09.2005	:	CMP allowed P.A. of both
14.10.2005	:	P.A. of both
24.11.2005	:	No sitting, P.A. of Complainant
24.11.2005	:	P.A. Opposite 1 filed for P.A. of Complainant
28.12.2005	:	P.A. complainant filed for W.A.
03.02.2006	:	Proof Affidavit of Opposite 2
08.03.2006	:	P.A. Opposite filed for W.A.
06.04.2006	:	W.A. (written argument)
17.05.2006	:	W.A.
19.06.2006	:	W.A.
28.07.2006	:	W.A.
25.08.2006	:	W.A. filed by complainant W.A. of Opposite Party
26.09.2006	:	W.A. filed by complainant W.A. of Opposite Party
15.11.2006	:	W.A. filed by complainant W.A. of Opposite Party

The Government of India from time-to-time have studied the problems of the consumers and taken remedial measures by enacting welfare legislations for protecting the interest of the consumers, and in the process enacted at different times a series of consumer protection laws.

The Consumer Protection Act has opened up an opportunity of easy, cheap and quick remedies for redressal of the grievances and the consumer movement has gained momentum and impetus. The lowest tribunal under the Act is the District Forum. Higher valuation matters have been given to State Commission and National Commission. The State Commission will hear and decide appeal from the orders of the District Forum. The National Commission in turn will hear and decide appeal from the order of the State Commission. Appeal from the order of the National Commission may be preferred to the Supreme Court.

The Forums may pass an order directing the opposite party to comply with one or more of the following:

1. to remove the defect from the goods pointed out by the appropriate laboratory;
2. to replace the goods with new goods of similar description free from any defect;
3. to return to the complainant the price, or as the case may be, the charges paid by the complainant; and
4. to pay such amount as may be awarded by it as compensation to the consumer for any loss or injury suffered due to the negligence of the opposite party.

An order made by the Forum shall be signed by all the members constituting it and, if there is any difference of opinion, the order of the majority of the members constituting it shall be the order of the Forum.

Every order made by the District Forum, the State Commission or the National Commission as the case may be, in the same manner as if it were a decree or order made by a court in a suit pending therein and it shall be lawful for the District Forum, the State Commission or the National Commission to send, in the event of its inability to execute it, such order to the court within the local limits of whose jurisdictions in the case of an order against a company where the registered office of the company is situated; or in the case of an order against any other person, the place where the person concerned voluntarily resides or carries on business or personally works for gain; is situated and thereupon, the court to which the order is so sent, shall execute the order as if it were a decree or order sent to it of execution.

Guidelines for Payment of Court Fees

Sl. No.	*District Forum*	*Court Fees*
1.	Upto 1 lakh	Nil
2.	Above 1 lakh to 5 lakhs	Rs. 200
3.	Above 5 lakhs to 10 lakhs	Rs. 400
4.	Above 10 lakhs to 20 lakhs	Rs. 500
	State Commission	
6.	Above 20 lakhs to 50 lakhs	Rs. 2000
7.	Above 50 lakhs to 1 crore	Rs. 4000
	National Commission	
8.	Above 1 crore	Rs. 5000

Thus the law has made elaborate provisions with regard to consumers, their rights and remedies. And it seems that the objects sought to be achieved have been substantially achieved. Now the consumers have much better protective weapons in their hands.

It is pertinent to note that as per the C.P. Act 1986, the General Policy of the Forum being constituted is also for speedy adjudication and disposal of the Consumers seeking Redressal of their grievances within a period of Six Months. Not withstanding this due to the heavy burden cost upon them and due to piling up of cases most of the complaint are being dragged on for more than 2 years.

PART VI

Consumer Rights and Their Protection

Chapter 12

Redressal of Supply Service Deficiency in Public Distribution System/ Fair Price Shops

R. ELANGOVAN

Nearly 36 percentage of Indian population live below poverty line and much depend on fair price shops or ration shops for their food supply. Administratively, most of the Indian state governments find it very difficult to manage supply of essential foods to needy people. There were reports of massive corruption taking place in every Fair Price Shop (FPS) in the country and there are known links between the local politicians and FPS owners. The distribution of food can be well come under 'service' of the governments. This is one service sector where one can find numerous complaints and the prevalence of ignorance among poor people to report the matter to the higher officials. Now many consumer forums are up in the arm to make complaints against PDS in the context of its service deficiency. The chapter highlights the existing redressal mechanisms to resolve the problems faced by consumers in Public Distribution System (PDS).

The main aim of the public distribution system is to ensure food security to all citizens, particularly to the poor people, by distributing essential commodities of good quality at reasonable prices every month through the fair price shops which are easily accessible.

During the time of World War II, the then British Government introduced the first structured public distribution of cereals in India through the rationing system—sale of a fixed quantity of ration (rice or wheat) to entitled families (ration cardholders) in specified cities/ towns. The Department of Food, under the Government of India, was created in 1942 to co-ordinate this arrangement. When the War ended, India, like many other countries, abolished the rationing system in 1943.

The Government had to reintroduce rationing in 1950 because of acute food shortage and declining food production. India retained public distribution of foodgrains as a deliberate social policy, when it embarked on the path of planned economic development in 1951. In the First Plan, the system, which was essentially urban-based till then, was extended to all such rural areas which suffered from chronic food shortages. Towards the end of the First Plan (1956), rationing had started losing its relevance due to comfortable foodgrains Availability. Thanks to the Green Revolution which resulted in self-sufficiency in food requirements for the Indian growing population.

However, true to its cyclic nature, food production dropped in 1958, when the Second Plan had just commenced. This forced the Government to restart the procurement of foodgrain and cereals and impose control on trading of foodgrains. It also decided to re-introduce PDS. Public Distribution System (PDS) is one of the systems for improving food security at the household level. PDS is a food subsidy programme comprising about half the total spending on anti-poverty programmes by the Central Government—explicitly targeted towards the poor. PDS ensures availability of essential commodities like rice, wheat, sugar, edible oils and kerosene to the consumers through a network of outlets, fair price stabilization and as an alternative channel to provide trade. PDS is effective in transferring foodgrains from surplus areas to few deficit regions. Later the programme was strengthened, improved and renamed the 'targeted public distribution system' or TPDS. The food stamp is also introduced on a pilot basis in selected districts in few states from 2004-05.

The creation of the Food Corporation of India and the Agricultural Prices Commission in 1965 consolidated the position of the PDS. The Government was now committed to announce a minimum support price for wheat and paddy and procure quantities that could not fetch even such minimum prices in the market. Foodgrains thus procured were to be used to maintain distribution through the PDS with a portion used to create and maintain buffer stocks. PDS was sustained as a deliberate social policy of the Government with the objectives of:

- Providing foodgrains and other essential items to vulnerable sections of society at reasonable (subsidised) prices;

- Having a moderating influence on the open market prices of cereals, the distribution of which constitutes a fairly big share of the total marketable surplus; and
- Ensuring equity in the matter of distribution of essential commodities.

In short, PDS, from mere rationing, had evolved into the National Food Security System.

General Problems of PDS

1. *Inadequacy of Quantity*: Initially, in the TPDS, each BPL family was entitled to only 10 kg of grain per month. This was clearly too low an allocation in relation to monthly needs. The allocation was raised to 20 kg per month in the Budget of March 2001. It has been raised from March 2002 to 35 kg per household for both BPL (Below Poverty Line) and APL (Above Poverty Line) families. According to the Indian Council of Medical Research, a person requires about 11 kg of cereals per month (or 330 gm per day). A family of five members would typically require 55 kg per month.
2. *Poor Qualities*: There has been frequent reporting in the press of the poor quality of grain received by households from the ration shops. The CAG Report also notes the poor quality of foodgrain supplied providing specific instances of the distribution of substandard grain. While the Food Corporation of India (FCI) does have a system of quality checks, some of the mechanisms seem to be not in use.
3. *Unsatisfactory Administrations*: A targeted programme requires more and better administration than a general universal programme. The reports of the CAG and other accounts of mistreating and poor administration of the TPDS indicate that the new administrative tasks have not been undertaken satisfactorily.
4. Lack of Information and Absence of Grievance Redressal System, Targeted Public Distribution System (TPDS) has increased the information requirements and flows of the system. This has not only added to administrative problems

but is likely to have affected consumers too. The CAG report, for instance, states that consumers have paid excess charges, that is, prices higher than announced. The lack of information among consumers on the appropriate prices may have helped those who charged a higher price. The CAG beneficiary study also found a problem of non-awareness of entitlements among consumers. The study reported the absence of grievance redressal systems.

5. *Refusal of States to Issue Cards to the Destitute*: Several states refuse to issue rations cards to the urban destitute including urban homeless, migrant labour, destitute women, children etc. due to lack of proof of address.

What are Rations?

Rations are the monthly quotas of certain essential commodities distributed at special rates to ration card holders by the government under the Public Distribution System (PDS). Rations are essential for people with limited incomes hence cardholders need to know their rights and assert them in order to get their rations regularly. The purpose of the Public Distribution System is to exercise some control over prices of essential foodgrains and commodities in the open market ensure supply of these to the average citizen for those living below the poverty line (BPL). For adivasis and people living below the poverty line, the government subsidises the cost of essential commodities, thus further reducing prices for these sections. But in some areas these ration are not made avilable to them.

Rationing Rules and Card Holders Rights

1. *The weekly quota is not forfeited if not purchased*: For the convenience of consumer who cannot buy the fortnightly quote at one time, purchase of rations on a weekly basis is permitted. If a card holder cannot purchase his ıations in the first fortnight of a month, he can do so in the second. Sugar is available owing to shortage or strikes by shopkeepers, truckers or godown employees in a particular month, these quotas will be made available in the next month by the government.

2. *Display of samples*: Samples of foodgrains, etc are to be displayed in sealed plastic bags. The general impression that rations are of poor quality is not correct. They have to be clean. The state government is supposed to lift stocks from the Food Corporation of India only after proper examination. It does not accept spoilt stocks. If the grains are of bad quality you have a right to complain and have then exchanged. Samples of the available foodgrains have to be displayed in the ration shops in sealed plastic bags bearing the number of the godown and the date of delivery. The cardholder can compare the quote given to him with the sample in the bag and ensure that he is given the same quality. If samples are displayed in plates you could be cheated.
3. *Ensure that you get a receipt*: The receipt is yellow in colour and in simple language. If the figures are not clear ask the shopkeeper to write them down legibly. The receipt should give the date of purchase, details of the rations supplied and the number of the ration shop in Marathi only. There is no rule that the ration can be purchased only once a day. You may make more purchase separately on the same day.
   If the shopkeeper has no change, ask him to write the amount due on the back of your receipt and to sign below so that the amount can be adjusted against your next bill.
4. You are entitled to buy only the commodities you require. The shopkeeper cannot insist that you buy wheat or rice in order to get your quota of kerosene or sugar.
5. A fee of Rs. 5 is charged for new card. The fee for replacement of a lost card is Rs. 10. There is no charge for issuing a temporary card, or for adding or deleting names in the ration card.
6. When applying for a new card or adding names to a card, verification will be carried out after your application is received and the card will be made available within 10 days.
7. To obtain a ration card, applicants do not need to have a fixed residence. Tenants, sub-tenants, pavement dwellers, temporary construction workers, contract labours and hostels can all obtain ration cards after inspection to verify

produce a "no objection" certificate from the owner of the premises.

8. If a card holder is moving from one locality of Chennai to another, there is no need to surrender his card. A slip giving the address of the rationoing office for the new residence, reference number and the number of the new ration shop (ARS No.) will be attached to his ration card by the rationing office. The card holder should first go to his change of residence; the officer-in-change will guide him regarding the steps to be taken.
9. If the card holder is moving to Chennai from distrcts or from outside the state, he will have to get a surrender slip from his old rationing office and present it at the new rationing office. If the card holder did not have a ration card in his former home he will have to get a certificate from the 'talathi' of his district to this effect. In case where documentary evidence cannot be produced, the Rationing Inspector will inspect the home, verify the statement of the applicant and issue a temporary card.
10. Card holders should not be intimated by threats made by the shopkeeper. He has no powers to seize, change or cancel their cards.

Information to be Displayed

It is mandatory for the fair price shops to publish the quantity of ration to be distributed, rate and stock for the card holders' information, according to the citizen's charter of the Food and Civil Supplies Department. But in reality, most of the fair price shops, particularly those in rural areas, fix rates on their own.

The ration shop has to display:

(a) the registration number of the ration shop (ARS No.).
(b) the number, address and phone number of the ration office.
(c) the inspector's name and the time of his weekly visit.
(d) the stock position of all rationed commodities in units.
(e) the official price list.
(f) the total number of ration cards registered with the shop.
(g) the total number of units.

A complaints book has to be available to card holders.

In order to ensure more transparency in Public Distribution System, all the District Collectors have been directed to give a press release every month indicating the allotment of various commodities made for Public Distribution System. They have also been requested to give the names of Kerosene wholesalers and the quantum of allotment given to each wholesalers. This information will be made available to all the District Panchayats and panchayat Union by the District Supply Officer of the district concerned. Details of allotment made to the shops will be made available by the Collectors to all the elected representatives of the area concerned namely MPs., MLAs. District Panchayat Presidents and members, etc. The District Collectors have been directed to arrange for the publication in the local Tamil Newspaper having wide circulation in their area, shop-wise details of the allotment made of different commodities and their off-take during the month. This will be done for one taluk at a time and will be done on a continuous basis.

How to Lodge a Complaint?

Quite often, kerosene, wheat and rice are not available or the sugar is less than 500 grams. People wish to complain against the shopkeeper but are afraid that he may be abusive or confiscate their card. At such times to whom should one complain? First, one should ask for the complaint book in the ration shop and enter the complaint in the book. Then inspector examines the book every time he visits the shop. If the inspector does not redress your complaint, you should complaint to the tehsildar/rationing officer. If there is still no action on the complaint then refer it to the Collector/Addl. Collector or District Supply Officer/Controller of Rationing. Regarding Policy matters, suggestions or complaints should be sent to the Secretary, Department of Foods Civil Supplies and Consumer Affairs or to the Minister. To ensure implementation of the rules and assert one's rights is difficult for one person; hence it is necessary to from local organizations of ration card holders. Local groups, women's groups and party branches should take the lead in solving card holder's problems. For this, complaints redressal committees need to be set up. Card holder, ration shopkeepers and ration inspector should be member of these committees.

Under Right to Information Act, 2005 the state civil supplies authorities are entrusted with the responsibilities of redressing the grievances of the card holders. The petitions and other letters from the public, that are received in person will be registered at once and acknowledgement given immediately. The petitions received by post will be acknowledged within 5 days. Final replies will be sent to the petitioners within 90 days.

Suggestions for Improvement

Some suggestions for improvement in the functioning of PDS are given below:

(i) Delivery of Stocks to FPSs should be on actual and not on sample wieghment.

(ii) Retail price at FPSs should be uniform throughout the state/ area.

(iii) Regular supply of good quality grains has to be ensured.

(iv) Entitlement card's easy availability and improvement in its design and durability.

(v) Open house debate for redressal of common grievances of the card holders at least once in a month.

(vi) Prominent display of competent authorities and appellate authorities where complaints can be lodge.

REFERENCES

Ahluwalia, Deepak (1993). 'Public Distribution of Food in India: Coverage, Targeting and Leakages'. *Food Policy*, Vol. 18, No. 1.

Government of India (1997). Focus on the Poor (Guidelines for the Implementation of the Targeted Public Distribution System), Ministry of Civil Supplies, Consumer Affairs and Public Distribution.

Government of Tamil Nadu, Policy note on Civil Supplies, 2005.

Jharwal, S.M. (1999). *Public Distribution System in India Reassessed*, Manak Publications, New Delhi.

Tyagi, D.S. (1990). *Managing India's Food Economy: Problems and Alternatives*, Sage Publications, New Delhi.

Chapter 13

Role of Government in Protecting Rights of Consumers in Service Sector

MYTHILI K. RAJENDRAN

Introduction

Service Sector in India is developing by leaps and bounds as it is being opened up to private and international players like:

- Transport (Aviation Sector especially),
- Electricity,
- Banking,
- Insurance, and
- Telecommunication.

Increase in purchasing power and growing consumerism have given additional impetus to Service Sector. Is Consumerism met with appropriate of just assurances and quality services from the service sector is the Question before us.

To analyze the role of the Government and suggest enhancement of its role, one has to understand the profile of consumers in India. The profile of Indian consumer is complete varied. There are informed rich people, uninformed rich people, informed poor and uninformed poor. There is unbalance in economic terms, educational levels, and legaly gaining power. So the Government has called upon itself to play a role of promoting just of equitable, sustainable, economic socially acceptable consumerism.

How does Government do it?

Government should ensure production and distributor and marketing shall by responsible to the needs and desires of the consumers.

- Curb exploitative lecesuniss practices which are rampant in the age of consumerism.
- To develop independent consumer groups, that would advocate rights of the consumers.
- To make consumer protection as the underlying principle behind all international trade registrations.
- To encourage market practices which provide consumers with variety of choice at lower price.

Consumer protection policies of the Government in line with requirements of government suggest there is a shooting consumer's protection policy.

Underlying Tenets such Policy are:

- Health and Safety of the consumers,
- Protection and promotion of Economic interests of the consumer,
- Safeguard consumer's right to information,
- Consumer education,
- Grievance redressal, and
- What has Government done so far?

What has Government done so far?

Government of India passed Consumer Protection Act in 1986. Though there were many laws prior to 1986 to protect the interests of the Consumer CP Act was unique for two reasons:

- It provided for compensation to the affected.
- It enabled setting up exclusive judicial forum to handle consumer related cases.

Some of the legislations which existed prior to 1986 are:

- Sale of Indian Products Act (1930)

- Agricultural Produce Act (1937)
- Minerals Act (1946).
- Prevention of Food Adulteration Act (1940)
- Pesticides Act (1968)
- Essential Commodities Act (1955 & 1974.)
- Companies Act (1956)
- Consumer and Trade Marks Act (1958)
- Patent Act (1970)
- Weights and Measures Act (1976)
- Household Electrical Appliances Act (1981-88)

Of these Drugs and Cosmetic Act, Prevention of Food Adulteration Act, Essential Commodities Act, Weights and Measures Act alone could bring the erring to look and furnish them.

As requested under the Consumer Protection Act. Government has set up judicial forums in districts, in state capitals and at national level to provide effective grievance redressal.

1. District Forum with a District Judge (Retd or Serving), 2 Members (1 to be a woman), Appellate jurisdiction.
2. State Forum, High Court Judge (Retd or Serving), 3 Member/ woman.
3. National Forum, Supreme Court of India, Supreme Court Judge has powers to entertain appeal on orders of national forum. (Retd or Serving) 5 members, Appellate Jurisdiction.

Apart from above there are also:

(a) Insurance sector has evolved a third party claim administration mechanism as a complement to growing consumers.
(b) There are special tribunals of motor vehicle claims.
(c) Oil complains have set up third party checking system to prevent adulteration of petroleum products.
(d) Electricity board has an independent in the line of finance and insurance companies now.
(e) The latest area to sting to the consumers against redtaps in service sector is the Right to Information Act.
(f) Government has also set up vigilance communities at micro

level and NGOs are part of periodical mandatory nettings at district, state and national levels.

(g) Standardization of services and products is yet another area taken up by the government to protect the interests of the consumers.

(h) Standardization of food such as milk, water is mandatory.

(i) Standardization of household common electric appliances is mandatory.

(j) Consumers are given choice of selecting standardized products with respect to silk, gold, wool, and other food products.

(k) Education of Consumers.

(l) Government has set-up consumer clubs in schools and colleges and roped in Self-Help Groups to samities the rural and urban population on effective consumerism through programmes like Jagriti Shivir Yojana.

(m) Government encourages setting up of VCOs.

(n) To set up a Consumer Forum. 7 persons have to come together and register. They are authorized in government sponsored programmes and meetings and represent before consumer courts.

Tasks before Government

To Encourage Sustainable Consumers: To develop and maintain mechanism which would enable exchange of information on national policies and measures in the field of consumer protection so that protectionist policies of one country does not become detrimental to that of another.

Chapter 14

Consumer Rights in Service Sector

S. GANGA BAI

The enactment of Consumer Law is aimed to protect the interest of Consumer and to exercise his rights as a responsible consumer. In the wake of liberalization several service sectors in various fields have emerged. The economic advancement of people contributed to the rapid growth of service organizations like private banking, insurance, communications, transport etc. These service sectors must provide proper dispensation of service and for which the consumer will have to be properly apprised of their legitimate entitlement in a transparent manner. The Consumer Protection is therefore playing a crucial role in ensuring this Service.

It is not denied that Consumer Fora's established under the Consumer Protection Act play an effective role in landmark judgments; these have been passed providing relief to consumers in the areas of banking, insurance, telecommunications, etc. The expansion of service-providers has added to the burden of Consumer Fora's to render justice to consumers. Since then, there has been a considerable delay in awarding compensation due to the heavy receipts of complaints and poor infrastructure. If every deficient service has to be represented to the Consumer Forum, the executives in the administration have no role to play.

The consumer awareness programme in its expanded activity provides programme in schools. The programme to such awareness activity should be extended to colleges also as more and more people come to know about their rights and privileges. The consumer awareness programme must also be designed in such a way to impart its implications in every field of service-providers instead of confining awareness programme in a general way. This definitely would help the people to know the deficiency in a particular sector and to approach for relief. The effective programme may also be conducted in rural and semi urban areas to benefit the rural and semi-urban people.

Hence, it suffices to highlight the need to equip the fora's with adequate infrastructure and presiding officers. Currently, the Consumer Fora's comprises of a Judge from legal fraternity like District Judge and two other members within the age group of 35 years with a degree qualifications with ability, integrity coupled 10 years of experience in handling problems relating to economics, law, commerce, accountancy, public affairs and administration. These officers are nominated by the Government. Though these qualifications it helps to assess the service-provider's deficiencies, the new challenges posed by the new service-providers in the field of telecom, banking, medical, etc. Even then call for greater in-depth study to judge these new sectors are needed.

It is appropriate to state how the word 'deficiency' is explained in the Consumer Protection Act. 'Deficiency' means any fault, imperfection, or shortcoming or inadequacy in the quality, nature and manner of performance which is required to be maintained by or under any law for the time being in force, has been undertaken to be performed by a person in pursuance of a contract or otherwise in relation to any service.

Here, the service consideration includes all services including medical and legal also. In the case of medical, normally the medical profession will totally resist any deficiency saying that they have given the best treatment in accordance with the ailment of the persons concerned. Therefore, unless the consumer has the basic medical knowledge he/she may not able to pin-point the deficiency. Therefore consumer groups have to educate the consumers in the medical field to educate him on the basic knowledge in medicine. In the case of legal profession there are instances where the legal fraternity failed to render their services in manner expected. At present the only source of action open to clients in such deficiencies is to report the same to the Bar Council for appropriate action. This has created a piquant situation where this category of service-providers used to escape without their services to the expectation of consumers.

In the case of Public Sector Organizations like oil companies, electricity, water board, etc, there is ever growing demand of their services. Ignoring the legitimate rights of the people for want of adequate machinery to deal with services, the public requires and deserves special attention. This should be addressed. Though there are internal agencies to redress the grievances of public the services are far from satisfactory and many people continue to agitate for better services.

There are instances where there exists non-execution of consumer Fora's orders by opposite party and also by the law enforcing authorities. This inaction used is to defeat the very purpose of the Act. Therefore, such inaction should not be allowed if we have to obtain the real benefit of Consumer Protection Laws. If the opposite party failed to comply with the orders of the Consumer Fora's or by the law enforcing authorities, such non-execution of orders will have to be treated has contempt of Court and a cognizable non-bailable offence. A time limit should also be fixed for execution of orders and also to minimize the delays. The provision contained in Clause 27 of the Consumer Protection Act will have to be invoked to comply with the orders if the time schedule is not adhered to.

Apart form this, another area which needs to be addressed is effective action related to luring the Public with substandard products through deceptive advertisements. This should also be considered as deficiency in service under the Consumer Protection Act. This will be of immense help to consumers who fall a victim to such deceptive techniques.

Chapter 15

Deficiency of Services in Banking Sector and Customer's Rights

S. RAVISHANKAR

Banking Sector in India is assuming a very significant role for national economic development. Apart from indigenous bank today we can find more foreign banks catering to the financial needs of Indian population. In the context of privatization and liberalization, the role of bank in the economic life of people becomes a vital factor. Therefore, banking service considered being important and every step are taken to rectify the general problems encountered by the customers in relations to banking service. This chapter makes an attempt to present the Ombudsman like bodies evolved by the Reserve Bank of India to redressal of customer's problems. Any aggrieved person can approach the banking Ombudsman to resolve their issues in relation to banking services. A modest attempt is also made to cite some important cases that were resolved by various redressal mechanisms to satisfy Customers/Consumers.

Banking in India has its origin as early as the vedic period. It is believed that the transistion from money lending to banking must have occurred even before Manu, the great Hindu Jurist, who has devoted a section of his work to deposits and advances and laid down rules relating to rates of interest. During the Mogul period, the indegenous bankers played a very important role in lending money and financing foreign trade and commerce. During the days of the East India Company, it was the turn of the agency houses to carry on the banking business. The General Bank of India was the first Joint Stock Bank to be established in the year 1786. The others which followed were the Bank of Hindustan and the Bengal Bank. The Bank of Hindustan is reported to have continued till 1906 while the other two failed in the meantime. In the first half of the 19th century the East India Company established three banks; the Bank of Bengal in 1809, the Bank of Bombay in 1840 and the Bank of Madras in 1843. These three banks also known as Presidency Banks, were independent units and functioned well. These three banks were amalgamated in 1920 and a new bank, the Imperial Bank of India was established on 27th January 1921. With the passing of the State Bank of India Act in 1955 the undertaking of the Imperial Bank of India was taken over by the newly constituted State Bank of India. The Reserve Bank which is the Central Bank was created in 1935 by passing Reserve Bank of India Act 1934. In the wake of the Swadeshi Movement, a number of banks with Indian management were established in the country, namely, Punjab National Bank Ltd, Bank of India Ltd, Canara Bank Ltd, Indian Bank Ltd, the Bank of Baroda Ltd, the Central Bank of India Ltd. On July 19, 1969, 14 major banks of the country were nationalised and in 15th April 1980 six more commercial private sector banks were also taken over by the government.

Types of Banks in India

Public Sector Banks

1. State Bank of India and its associate banks called the State Bank group
2. 20 Nationalized Banks
3. Regional Rural Banks mainly sponsored by Public Sector Banks

Private Sector Banks

1. Old Generation Private Banks
2. New Generation Private Banks
3. Foreign Banks in India
4. Scheduled Co-operative Banks
5. Non-Scheduled Banks

Co-operative Sector

The co-operative banking sector has been developed in the country to supplement the village money-lender. The co-operatiev banking sector in India is divided into 4 components

1. State Co-operative Banks
2. Central Co-operative Banks
3. Primary Agriculture Credit Societies
4. Land Development Banks
5. Urban Co-operative Banks
6. Primary Agricultural Development Banks
7. Primary Land Development Banks
8. State Land Development Banks

Development Banks

1. Industrial Finance Corporation of India (IFCI)
2. Industrial Development Bank of India (IDBI)
3. Industrial Credit and Investment Corporation of India (ICICI)
4. Industrial Investment Bank of India (IIBI)
5. Small Industries Development Bank of India (SIDBI)
6. SCICI Ltd.
7. National Bank for Agriculture and Rural Development (NABARD)
8. Export Import Bank of India
9. National Housing Bank

The Disputes Redressal Agencies (District Forums, State Commissions and National Commission) under the Consumer Protection Act, 1986 adjudicate upon the complaints of consumers relating to defaults in products and deficiency in service. 'Service' as defined in the Act includes the provision of facilities in connection with banking. The decisions of the State Commissions, the National Commission, and the Supreme Court (as the final authority), on different aspects of banking and other services offered by banks have been reported in various law journals. A short compilation of the decisions from 1995 to 2005 has been made with a view to giving a brief account of the principles laid down in these cases. Each case is given separately along with the citation for enabling access to the full text of the case, whenever necessary.

The principles laid down by the various decisions of the Consumer Commissions and the Supreme Court and included in the compilation can be summarized as under:

(i) Failure/Delay in Repaying Deposits

Withholding of the amount due on a fixed deposit after its maturity, amounts to deficiency in service. Delayed payment of term deposits on maturity also amounts to deficiency in service. The principle applies to cases of inordinate delay in payment of proceeds of premature encashment of deposits as well.

(ii) Payment and Collection of Cheques/Drafts

Wrongful dishonour of cheques due to the negligence or mistake on the part of the bank has been held to amount deficiency in service. Dishonour of DDs due to the lapse or omission on the part of the officials of the bank like non-affixation of signatures, failure to mention code number etc. have also been held to be amounting to deficiency in service.

(iii) Loans and Advances

Refusal to Grant Loans

Matters concerning the eligibility of parties to any credit assistance, viability of the project and continuation of the credit facilities or the operation of the account by any party, are within the discretion of the financial institution/bank depending upon various factors like financial discipline and past history of borrower and his ability to pay the loan, if such discretion is exercised *bonafide*. Even though the bank has the right to refuse or grant loan, causing undue delay in releasing the instalments of the sanctioned loan might be held to amount to deficiency in service.

Interest

Charging interest at a rate higher than the rate stipulated in the loan agreement would also amount to deficiency in service. Interest cannot be claimed in a consumer case under Section 34 of the Code of Civil Procedure as these provisions are not applicable. However, based on the underlying principles of justice, equity and good conscience, the Forums and Commissions can grant appropriate interest in each case. Although banks cannot give interest exceeding that prescribed by the Reserve Bank, they have a duty to inform the depositor about this, the failure of which, would amount to deficiency in service.

(iv) Security for Loans

Non-return of Documents

Banks are liable for deficiency in service in cases were they fail to return the security documents even after repayment of the whole loan.

Insurance of Security

Banks are not bound to insure the security taken for a loan unless the loan agreement provides for insurance and as such, failure to insure does not amount to deficiency in service. Further, merely because the owner of a vehicle has given the cheque for insurance premium to the bank along with monthly instalment of loan taken for purchase of the vehicle, liability arising out of an accident to third parties cannot be shifted to the bank.

(v) Lien

Banks have a right to exercise lien under Section 171 of the Indian Contract Act against the dues from constituents/customers. However, the banks cannot exercise lien over the personal account of a customer on the ground that money was due to the bank in another account where he acts in a different capacity, if there is no agreement to that effect.

(vi) Bank Guarantee

The failure of a bank to honour bank guarantee is a deficiency in service. However, in cases where a demand was made not in accordance with the conditions of the guarantee and therefore, the guarantee was not honoured, it would not amount to deficiency in service.

(vii) Locker

A bank is liable for loss of articles kept in the locker with the bank. The bank cannot contract out of its responsibilities in relation to a locker by describing the agreement as that between a landlord and a tenant. When locker was found emptied and contents lost, the banks have been held liable for deficiency in service. However, in some such cases, the disputes were left open to be decided by the Civil Court after taking detailed evidence.

(viii) Security in Bank's Premises

A Bank is responsible for deficiency in service for lack of security in its premises and loss caused to customers accordingly. This is on the ground that ensuring the safety of the money to be deposited and/or withdrawn inside the bank premises is implicitly a part of the service rendered by a bank to a customer.

(ix) Consumer Forum—Jurisdiction and Procedure

A consumer complaint may not be entertained by the Consumer Forums when the matter is subjudice before a competent Civil Court.

A person who acts as surety for another and does not hire/avail service from the bank, is not a consumer of the bank and therefore, his complaint may not be entertained.

(x) Voluminous Evidence—Complicated Questions of Law and Fact

In cases involving complex questions of facts and interpretation of laws and rights and obligations of parties under various Statutes, the complainants have to seek redressal of their grievances before Civil Courts not the Consumer Forum. Similar is the case when elaborate evidence is required to be taken.

(xi) Limitation

A Bank may exercise lien under Section 171 of the Contract Act even where the debt is barred by limitation.

A consumer can initiate proceeding against a banker for non-release of securities even after the expiry of the period of limitation. This is based on the principle that the banker holds any goods as security from a customer as trustee and the security is not intended to be transferred to him, nor can he acquire any title to it, except on the basis of legal proceedings.

(xii) Other Banking Services

Operation of Account

The stoppage of operation of account of a partnership firm on account of an arbitration award and the subsequent legal opinions obtained by the bank would not amount to deficiency in service.

Closing of Account

Closing of account without the instructions of the account holder would amount to deficiency in service.

Refusal of Cheque Book

The refusal to provide cheque book facility to a customer on the ground of not maintaining the minimum balance in his account may not amount to deficiency in service.

Service Charges

An increase in charges levied by a bank for its services doe not fall within the provisions of the Consumer Protection Act. A bank may levy charges for issuance of MICR cheques, so long as it is not against the directives of the Reserve Bank of India. This cannot be termed 'unilateral' and taking the consent of each customer does not arise.

Rendering of Account

A demand for rendering of accounts of transactions with a bank is not within the scope of the provisions of the Consumer Protection Act.

Succession Certificate

It has been held that there is no deficiency in service on the part of a bank in insisting that the children of a deceased account holder should produce a succession certificate before releasing the amount to them in accordance with the Succession Act and the Reserve Bank guidelines.

Insistence on Denomination of Notes

A customer cannot as of right insist for a particular denomination of notes, as the notes provided by the bank are legal tender and therefore, no deficiency in service in failing to comply with the demand.

Forgery of Power of Attorney

Once a registered power of attorney is produced before the bank, the bank does not have to make any further verification of signature. As the bank is not expected to verify signature, it cannot be held responsible for negligence in verification of signature. The failure in respect of an act which does not form part of the service cannot be considered as a deficiency in service.

Compliance of RBI Directions

It has been held that the Consumer Forum may not direct the banks to make payment to a depositor contrary to the directions issued by RBI under section 35A of the Banking Regulation Act or allow the directions issued by RBI to be flouted.

Vicarious Libaility

A bank is bound by the act of negligence of its staff during the course of employment. Thus where the bank cashier fails to account for the money deposited with him at the counter, the bank would be liable.

Rude Behaviour

A bank may be held liable for deficiency in service owing to rude behaviour of its officials and be ordered to pay compensation for the mental agony and discomfort caused.

Notice before Auction

A notice to pay or face auction without making any earlier demand for repayment of loan and without giving date of auction was held to constitute deficiency in service.

Non-Return of Dishonoured Cheque

The failure to return a dishonoured cheque has been held to be deficiency in service where the complainant was unable to take action against the drawer without the instrument.

Strike

A bank may not be liable to pay compensation for suspension of business due to illegal strike by the employees and when no loss is caused due to the negligence of the bank. However, in a case when the strike by award staff was not such as to paralyse work and when the officers and other employees were willing to work and still the salary accounts were not credited, it was held that the bank was liable for deficiency in service.

Banking Service

The grant of relief of rendition of accounts in relation to transactions with the Bank is not within the scope of the provisions of the Consumer Protection Act and the averments in the petition do not make out any deficiency in the service rendered by the Bank. The rendition of accounts by the Bank and the recovery of amounts that may be found due as a result of settlement of accounts are reliefs that can be obtained only by recourse to a suit in the Civil Court. *M/s. House of Dubary vs. New Bank of India and Others,* 1991(1) CPR 216 (NC).

The bank is liable for deficiency in service for inordinate delays in providing banking services and the customer of the bank is entitled to claim compensation for the loss and the injury suffered by him due to the inordinate delay in the payment of the amount of deposit certificate on its premature encashment. *P.N. Prasad vs. Union Bank of India,* 1991(1) CPR 198 (SCDRC- AP, Hyderabad).

The banker is supposed to safeguard the interest of the depositors when his amount is entrusted to the custody of the Bank and the Bank is liable to return the amount with interest. In the absence of any directions from the customer, no banker can unilaterally and arbitrarily transfer the money of a depositor from his account and deposit in the account of another customer. This amounts to deficiency in service by the bank. *Dilip Madhukar Kambli vs. Nilesh Vasant*

Borkar and Others, 1991(1) CPR 571(SCDRC-New Bombay, Maharashtra).

The Commission ruled that adopting discriminatory practice in sanctioning loan without basis by the cooperative society or Bank amounts to deficiency in service and such practice is liable to be stopped. *Madras Prov. Consumer Association vs. The Registrar Coop. Societies, Madras and Others (Madras),* 1991(2) CPR 447 (SCDRC-Madras).

APPENDICES

Appendix I

Consumer Protection Act, 1986

[Act No. 68 of Year 1986, dated 24th December, 1986]

An Act to provide for better protection of the interests of consumers and for that purpose to make provision for the establishment of consumer councils and other authorities for the settlement of consumers' disputes and for matters connected therewith

Be it enacted by Parliament in the Thirty-seventh Year of the Republic of India as follows:

Chapter	*Sections*	*Title*
I	1-3	Preliminary
II	4-8	Consumer Protection Councils
III	9-27	Consumer Disputes Redressal Agencies
IV	28-31	Miscellaneous

CHAPTER I: PRELIMINARY

1. Short title, extent, commencement and applications

(1) This Act may be called the Consumer Protection Act, 1986.

(2) It extends to the whole of India except the State of Jammu and Kashmir.

(3) It shall come into force on such date as the Central Government may, by notification, appoint and different dates

may be appointed for different States and for different provisions of this Act.

(4) Save as otherwise expressly provided by the Central Government by notifications, this Act shall apply to all goods and services.

2. Definitions

(1) In this Act, unless the context otherwise requires,—

[1][(a) "**appropriate laboratory**" means a laboratory or organisation—

(i) recognised by the Central Government;

(ii) recognised by a State Government, subject to such guidelines as may be prescribed by the Central Government in this behalf; or

(iii) any such laboratory or organisation established by or under any law for the time-being in force, which is maintained, financed or aided by the Central Government or a State Government for carrying out analysis or test of any goods with a view to determining whether such goods suffer from any defect;

[2][(aa) "**branch office**" means—

(i) any establishment described as a branch by the opposite party, or

(ii) any establishment carrying on either the same or substantially the same activity as that carried on by the head office of the establishment;

(b) "**complainant**" means—

(i) a consumer; or

(ii) any voluntary consumer association registered under the Companies Act, 1956 (1 of 1956), or under any other law for the time being in force; or

(iii) the Central Government or any State Government,

[2][(iv) one or more consumers, where there are numerous consumers having the same interest;] who or which makes a complaint;

(c) "**complaint**" means any allegation in writing made by a complainant that—

[1][(i) an unfair trade practice or a restrictive trade practice has been adopted by any trader;]

(ii) [1][the goods bought by him or agreed to be bought by him] suffer from one or more defect;

(iii) [1][the services hired or availed of or agreed to be hired or availed of by him] suffer from deficiency in any respect;

(iv) a trader has charged for the goods mentioned in the complaint a price in excess of the price fixed by or under any law for the time being in force or displayed on the goods or any package containing such goods;

[2][(v) goods which will be hazardous to life and safety when used, are being offered for sale to the public in contravention of the provisions of any law for the time being in force requiring traders to display information in regard to the contents, manner and effect of use of such goods.With a view to obtaining any relief provided by or under this Act;

(d) "**consumer**" means any person who—

(i) buys any goods for a consideration which has been paid or promised or partly paid and partly promised, or under any system of deferred payment and includes any user of such goods other than the person who buys such goods for consideration paid or promised or partly paid or partly promised, or under any system of deferred payment when such use is made with the approval of such person, but does not include a person who obtains such goods for resale or for any commercial purpose; or

(ii) [1][hires or avails of] any services for a consideration which has been paid or promised or partly paid and partly promised, or under any system of deferred payment and includes any beneficiary of such services other than the person who [1][hires or avails of] the services for consideration paid or promised, or partly paid and partly promised, or under any system of deferred payments, when such services are availed of with the approval of the first-mentioned person;

[2][*Explanation*: For the purposes of sub-clause (i), "commercial purpose" does not include use by a consumer of goods bought and used by him exclusively for the purpose of earning his livelihood, by means of self-employment;]

(e) "**consumer dispute**" means a dispute where the person against whom a complaint has been made, denies or disputes the allegations contained in the complaint;

(f) "**defect**" means any fault, imperfection or shortcoming in the quality, quantity, potency, purity or standard which is required to be maintained by or under any law for the time being in force or [2][under any contract, express or] implied, or as is claimed by the trader in any manner whatsoever in relation to any goods;

(g) "**deficiency**" means any fault, imperfection, shortcoming or inadequacy in the quality, nature and manner of performance which is required to be maintained by or under any law for the time being in force or has been undertaken to be performed by a person in pursuance of a contract or otherwise in relation to any service;

(h) "**District Forum**" means a Consumer Disputes Redressal Forum established under clause (a) of Section 9;

(i) "**goods**" means goods as defined in the Sale of Goods Act, 1930 (3 of 1930);

(j) "**manufacturer**" means a person who—

(i) makes or manufactures any goods or parts thereof; or

(ii) does not make or manufacture any goods but assembles parts thereof made or manufactured by others and claims the end product to be goods manufactured by himself; or

(iii) puts or causes to be put his own mark on any goods made or manufactured by any other manufacturer and claims such goods to be goods made or manufactured by himself.

[*Explanation*: Where a manufacturer despatches any goods or part thereof to any branch office maintained by him, such branch office shall not be deemed to be the manufacturer even though the parts so despatched to it are assembled at such branch office and are sold or distributed from such branch office.]

[2][(jj) "**member**" includes the President and a member of the National Commission or a State Commission or a District Forum, as the case may be;]

(k) "**National Commission**" means the National Consumer Disputes Redressal Commission established under clause (c) of Section 9;

(l) "**notification**" means a notification published in the Official Gazette;

(m) "**person**" includes—

(i) a firm whether registered or not;

(ii) a Hindu undivided family;

(iii) a co-operative society;

(iv) every other association of persons whether registered under the Societies Registration Act, 1860 (22 of 1860) or not;

(n) "**prescribed**" means prescribed by rules made by the State Government, or as the case may be, by the Central Government under this Act;

[2][(nn) "**restrictive trade practice**" means any trade practice which requires a consumer to buy, hire or avail of any goods or, as the case may be, services as a condition precedent for buying, hiring or availing of other goods or services;]

(o) "**service**" means service of any description which is made available to potential users and includes the provision of facilities in connection with banking, financing, insurance, transport, processing, supply of electrical or other energy, boarding or lodging or both, [6][housing construction], entertainment, amusement or the purveying of news or other information, but does not include the rendering of any service free of charge or under a contract of personal service;

(p) "**State Commission**" means a Consumer Disputes Redressal Commission established in a State under clause (b) of Section 9;

(q) "**trader**" in relation to any goods means a person who sells or distributes any goods for sale and includes the manufacturer thereof, and where such goods are sold or distributed in package form, includes the packer thereof;

[2][(r) "**unfair trade practice**" means a trade practice which, for the purpose of promoting the sale, use or supply of any goods or for the provision of any service, adopts any unfair method or unfair or deceptive practice including any of the following practices, namely,—

(1) the practice of making any statement, whether orally or in writing or by visible representation which,—

(i) falsely represents that the goods are of a particular standard, quality, quantity, grade, composition, style or model;

(ii) falsely represents that the services are of a particular standard, quality or grade;

(iii) falsely represents any re-built, second-hand, renovated, reconditioned or old goods as new goods;

(iv) represents that the goods or services have sponsorship, approval, performance, characteristics, accessories, uses or benefits which such goods or services do not have;

(v) represents that the seller or the supplier has a sponsorship or approval or affiliation which such seller or supplier does not have;

(vi) makes a false or misleading representation concerning the need for, or the usefulness of, any goods or services;

(vii) gives to the public any warranty or guarantee of the performance, efficacy or length of life of a product or of any goods that is not based on an adequate or proper test thereof: Provided that where a defence is raised to the effect that such warranty or guarantee is based on adequate or proper test, the burden of proof of such defence shall lie on the person raising such defence;

(viii) makes to the public a representation in a form that purports to be—

(i) a warranty or guarantee of a product or of any goods or services; or

(ii) a promise to replace, maintain or repair an article or any part thereof or to repeat or continue a service until it has achieved a specified result,

if such purported warranty or guarantee or promise is materially misleading or if there is no reasonable prospect that such warranty, guarantee or promise will be carried out;

(ix) materially misleads the public concerning the price at which a product or like products or goods or services, have been or are, ordinarily sold or provided, and, for this purpose, a representation as to price shall be deemed to refer to the price at which the product or goods or services has or have been sold by sellers or provided by suppliers generally in the relevant market unless it is clearly the price at which the product has been sold or services have been provided by the person by whom or on whose behalf the representation is made;

(x) gives false or misleading facts disparaging the goods, services or trade of another person.

Explanation: For the purposes of clause (1), a statement that is—

(a) expressed on an article offered or displayed for sale, or on its wrapper or container; or

(b) expressed on anything attached to, inserted in, or accompanying, an article offered or displayed for sale, or on anything on which the article is mounted for display or sale; or

(c) contained in or on anything that is sold, sent, delivered, transmitted or in any other manner whatsoever made available to a member of the public,

shall be deemed to be a statement made to the public by, and only by, the person who had caused the statement to be so expressed, made or contained;

(2) permits the publication of any advertisement whether in any newspaper or otherwise, for the sale or supply at a bargain price, of goods or services that are not intended to be offered for sale or supply at the bargain price, or for a period that is, and in quantities that are, reasonable, having regard to the nature of the market in which the business is carried on, the nature and size of business, and the nature of the advertisement;.

Explanation: For the purposes of clause (2), "bargaining price" means—

(a) a price that is stated in any advertisement to be a bargain price, by reference to an ordinary price or otherwise, or

(b) a price that a person who reads, hears or sees the advertisement, would reasonably understand to be a bargain price having regard to the prices at which the product advertised or like products are ordinarily sold;

(3) permits—

(a) the offering of gifts, prizes or other items with the intention of not providing them as offered or creating impression that something is being given or offered free of charge when it is fully or partly covered by the amount charged in the transaction as a whole;

(b) the conduct of any contest, lottery, games of chance or skill, for the purpose of promoting, directly or indirectly, the sale, use or supply of any product or any business interest;

(4) permits the sale or supply of goods intended to be used, or are of a kind likely to be used, by consumers, knowing or having reason to believe that the goods do not comply with the standards prescribed by competent authority relating to performance, composition, contents, design, constructions, finishing or packaging as are necessary to prevent or reduce the risk of injury to the person using the goods;

(5) permits the hoarding or destruction of goods, or refuses to sell the goods or to make them available for sale or to provide any service, if such-hoarding or destruction or refusal raises or tends to raise or is intended to raise, the cost of those or other similar goods or services.

(2) Any reference in this Act to any other Act or provision thereof which is not in force in any area to which this Act applies shall be construed to have a reference to the corresponding Act or provision thereof in force in such area.

3. Act not in derogation of any other law. The provisions of this Act shall be in addition to and not in derogation of the provisions of any other law for the time being in force.

CHAPTER II: CONSUMER PROTECTION COUNCILS

4. The Central Consumer Protection Council

(1) The Central Government may, by notification, establish with effect from such date as it may specify in such notification, a council to be known as the Central Consumer Protection Council (hereinafter referred to as the Central Council).

(2) The Central Council shall consist of the following members, namely,—

(a) the Minister in charge of [1][consumer affairs] in the Central Government, who shall be its Chairman, and

(b) such number of other official or non-official members representing such interests as may be prescribed.

5. Procedure for meetings of the Central Council

(1) The Central Council shall meet as and when necessary, but [1][at least one meeting] of the council shall be held every year.

(2) The Central Council shall meet at such time and place as the Chairman may think fit and shall observe such procedure in regard to the transaction of its business as may be prescribed.

6. Objects of the Central Council

The objects of the Central Council shall be to promote and protect the rights of the consumers such as—

(a) the right to be protected against the marketing of goods [2][and services] which are hazardous to life and property;

(b) the right to be informed about the quality, quantity, potency, purity, standard and price of goods [1][or services, as the case may be], so as to protect the consumer against unfair trade practices;

(c) the right to be assured, wherever possible, access to a variety of goods and services at competitive prices;

(d) the right to be heard and to be assured that consumers' interests will receive due consideration at appropriate forums;

(e) the right to seek redressal against unfair trade practices [1][or restrictive trade practices] or unscrupulous exploitation of consumers; and

(f) the right to consumer education.

7. The State Consumer Protection Councils

(1) The State Government may, by notification, establish with effect from such date as it may specify in such notification, a council to be known as the Consumer Protection Council (hereinafter referred to as the State Council).

[1][(2) The State Council shall consist of the following members, namely—

(a) The Minister in-charge of consumer affairs in the State Government who shall be its Chairman;

(b) Such number of other official or non-official members representing such interests as may be prescribed by the State Government.

(3) The State Council shall meet as and when necessary but not less than two meetings shall be held every year.

(4) The State Council shall meet at such time and place as the

Chairman may think fit and shall observe such procedure in regard to the transaction of its business as may be prescribed by the State Government.

8. Objects of the State Council

The objects of every State Council shall be to promote and protect within the State the rights of the consumers laid down in clauses (a) to (f) of Section 6.

CHAPTER III: CONSUMER DISPUTES REDRESSAL AGENCIES

9. Establishment of Consumer Disputes Redressal Agencies

There shall be established for the purposes of this Act, the following agencies, namely—

(a) a Consumer Disputes Redressal Forum to be known as the "District Forum" established by the State Government [3][* * *] in each district of the State by notification:
[2][Provided that the State Government may, if it deems fit, establish more than one District Forum in a district;

(b) a Consumer Disputes Redressal Commission to be known as the "State Commission" established by the State Government [3][* * *] in the State by notification; and

(c) a National Consumer Disputes Redressal Commission established by the Central Government by notification.

10. Composition of the District Forum

[1][(1) Each District Forum shall consist of—

(a) a person who is, or has been, or is qualified to be a District Judge, who shall be its President;

(b) two other members, who shall be persons of ability, integrity and standing, and have adequate knowledge or experience of, or have shown capacity in dealing with, problems relating to economics, law, commerce, accountancy, industry, public affairs or administration, one of whom shall be a woman.

[2][(1A) Every appointment under sub-section (1) shall be made by the State Government on the recommendation of a selection committee consisting of the following, namely—

(i) The President of the State Commission—Chairman,
(ii) Secretary, Law Department of the State—Member,
(iii) Secretary in-charge of the Department dealing with consumer affairs in the State—Member.

(2) Every member of the District Forum shall hold office for a term of five years or up to the age of 65 years, whichever is earlier, and shall not be eligible for re-appointment:

Provided that a member may resign his office in writing under his hand addressed to the State Government and on such resignation being accepted, his office shall become vacant and may be filled by the appointment of a person possessing any of the qualifications mentioned in sub-section (1) in relation to the category of the member who has resigned.

(3) The salary or honorarium and other allowances payable to, and the other terms and conditions of service of the members of the District Forum shall be such as may be prescribed by the State Government.

11. Jurisdiction of the District Forum

(1) Subject to the other provisions of this Act, the District Forum shall have jurisdiction to entertain complaints where the value of the goods or services and the compensation, if any, claimed [1][does not exceed rupees five lakhs].

(2) A complaint shall be instituted in a District Forum within the local limits of whose jurisdiction—

(a) the opposite party or each of the opposite parties, where there are more than one, at the time of the institution of the complaint, actually and voluntarily resides or [1][carries on business, or has a branch office or] personally works for gain; or
(b) any of the opposite parties, where there are more than one, at the time of the institution of the complaint, actually and

voluntarily resides, or [1][carries on business or has a branch office, or personally works for gain:

Provided that in such case either the permission of the District Forum is given, or the opposite parties who do not reside, or [1][carry on business or have a branch office, or personally work for gain, as the case may be, acquiesce in such institution; or

(c) the cause of action, wholly or in part, arises.

[1][12. Manner in which complaint shall be made

A complaint in relation to any goods sold or delivered or agreed to be sold or delivered or any service provided or agreed to be provided, may be filed with a District Forum, by—

(a) the consumer to whom such goods are sold or delivered or agreed to be sold or delivered or such service provided or agreed to be provided;

(b) any recognised consumers association whether the consumer to whom the goods sold or delivered or service provided or agreed to be provided is a member of such association or not; or

(c) one or more consumers, where there are numerous consumers having the same interest, with the permission of the District Forum, on behalf of, or for the benefit of, all consumers so interested; or

(d) the Central or the State Government.

13. Procedure on Receipt of Complaint

(1) The District Forum shall, on receipt of a complaint, if it relates to any goods—

(a) refer a copy of the complaint to the opposite party mentioned in the complaint directing him to give his version of the case within a period of thirty days or such extended period not exceeding fifteen days as may be granted by the District Forum;

(b) where the opposite party on receipt of a complaint referred to him under clause (a) denies or disputes the allegations contained in the complaint, or omits or fails to take any action to represent his case within the time given by the District Forum, the District Forum shall proceed to settle the consumer dispute in the manner specified in clauses (c) to (g);

(c) where the complaint alleges a defect in the goods which cannot be determined without proper analysis or test of the goods, the District Forum shall obtain a sample of the goods from the complainant, seal it and authenticate it in the manner prescribed and refer the sample so sealed to the appropriate laboratory along with a direction that such laboratory make an analysis with a view to finding out whether such goods suffer from any defect alleged in the complaint or suffer from any other defect and to report its findings thereon to the District Forum within a period of forty-five days of the receipt of the reference or within such extended period as may be granted by the District Forum;

(d) before any sample of the goods is referred to any appropriate laboratory under clause (c), the District Forum may require the complainant to deposit to the credit of the Forum such fees as may be specified, for payment to the appropriate laboratory for carrying out the necessary analysis or test in relation to the goods in question;

(e) the District Forum shall remit the amount deposited to its credit under clause (d) to the appropriate laboratory to enable it to carry out the analysis or test mentioned in clause (c) and on receipt of the report from the appropriate laboratory, the District Forum shall forward a copy of the report along with such remarks as the District Forum may feel appropriate to the opposite party;

(f) if any of the parties disputes the correctness of the findings of the appropriate laboratory, or disputes the correctness of the methods of analysis or test adopted by the appropriate laboratory, the District Forum shall require the opposite party or the complainant to submit in writing his objections in regard to the report made by the appropriate laboratory;

(g) the District Forum shall thereafter give a reasonable opportunity to the complainant as well as the opposite party of being heard as to the correctness or otherwise of the report made by the appropriate laboratory and also as to the objection made in relation thereto under clause (f) and issue an appropriate order under Section 14.

(2) The District Forum shall, if the complaint received by it under Section 12 relates to goods in respect of which the procedure specified in sub-section (1) cannot be followed, or if the complaint relates to any services—

(a) refer a copy of such complaint to the opposite party directing him to give his version of the case within a period of thirty days or such extended period not exceeding fifteen days as may be granted by the District Forum;
(b) where the opposite party, on receipt of a copy of the complaint, referred to him under clause (a) denies or disputes the allegations contained in the complaint, or omits or fails to take any action to represent his case within the time given by the District Forum, the District Forum shall proceed to settle the consumer dispute—
    (i) on the basis of evidence brought to its notice by the complainant and the opposite party, where the opposite party denies or disputes the allegation contained in the complaint, or
    (ii) on the basis of evidence brought to its notice by the complainant where the opposite party omits or fails to take any action to represent his case within the time given by the Forum.

(3) No proceedings complying with the procedure laid down in sub-sections (1) and (2) shall be called in question in any court on the ground that the principles of natural justice have not been complied with.

(4) For the purposes of this section, the District Forum shall have the same powers as are vested in a civil court under the Code of Civil Procedure, 1908 (5 of 1908) while trying a suit in respect of the following matters, namely—

(i) the summoning and enforcing attendance of any defendant or witness and examining the witness on oath;

(ii) the discovery and production of any document or other material object producible as evidence;
(iii) the reception of evidence on affidavits;
(iv) the requisitioning of the report of the concerned analysis or test from the appropriate laboratory or from any other relevant source;
(v) issuing of any commission for the examination of any witness; and
(vi) any other matter which may be prescribed.

(5) Every proceeding before the District Forum shall be deemed to be a judicial proceeding within the meaning of Sections 193 and 228 of the Indian Penal Code (45 of 1860), and the District Forum shall be deemed to be a civil court for the purposes of Section 195 and Chapter XXVI of the Code of Criminal Procedure, 1973 (2 of 1974).

[2][(6) Where the complainant is a consumer referred to in sub-clause (iv) of clause (b) of sub-section (1) of Section 2, the provisions of Rule 8 of Order I of Schedule I to the Code of Civil Procedure, 1908 (5 of 1908) shall apply subject to the modification that every reference therein to a suit or decree shall be construed as a reference to a complaint or the order of the District Forum thereon.]

14. Finding of the District Forum

(1) If, after the proceeding conducted under Section 13, the District Forum is satisfied that the goods complained against suffer from any of the defects specified in the complaint or that any of the allegations contained in the complaint about the services are proved, it shall issue an order to the opposite party directing him to [1][do] one or more of the following things, namely—

(a) to remove the defect pointed out by the appropriate laboratory from the goods in question;
(b) to replace the goods with new goods of similar description which shall be free from any defect;
(c) to return to the complainant the price, or, as the case may be, the charges paid by the complainant;
(d) to pay such amount as may be awarded by it as compensation to the consumer for any loss or injury suffered by the consumer due to the negligence of the opposite party.

[2][(e) to remove the defects or deficiencies in the services in question;

(f) to discontinue the unfair trade practice or the restrictive trade practice or not to repeat them;

(g) not to offer the hazardous goods for sale;

(h) to withdraw the hazardous goods from being offered for sale;

(i) to provide for adequate costs to parties.]

[4][(2) Every proceeding referred to in sub-section (1) shall be conducted by the President of the District Forum and at least one member thereof sitting together:

Provided that where the member, for any reason, is unable to conduct the proceeding till it is completed, the President and the other member shall conduct such proceeding de novo:

(2A) Every order made by the District Forum under sub-section (1) shall be signed by its President and the member or members who conducted the proceedings:

Provided that where the proceeding is conducted by the President and one member and they differ on any point or points, they shall state the point or points on which they differ and refer the same to the other member for hearing on such point or points and the opinion of the majority shall be the order of the District Forum.

(3) Subject to the foregoing provisions, the procedure relating to the conduct of the members of the District Forum, its sittings and other matters shall be such as may be prescribed by the State Government.

15. Appeal

Any person aggrieved by an order made by the District Forum may prefer an appeal against such order to the State Commission within a period of thirty days from the date of the order, in such form and manner as may be prescribed:

Provided that the State Commission may entertain an appeal after the expiry of the said period of thirty days if it is satisfied that there was sufficient cause for not finding it within that period.

16. Composition of the State Commission

(1) Each State Commission shall consist of—

(a) a person who is or has been a Judge of a High Court, appointed by the State Government, who shall be its President:

[2][Provided that no appointment under this clause shall be made except after consultation with the Chief Justice of the High Court.

(b) two other members, who shall be persons of ability, integrity and standing and have adequate knowledge or experience of, or have shown capacity in dealing with, problems relating to economics, law, commerce, accountancy, industry, public affairs or administration, one of whom shall be a woman:

[2][Provided that every appointment under this clause shall be made by the State Government on the recommendation of a selection committee consisting of the following, namely—

(i) President of the State Commission—Chairman,

(ii) Secretary of the Law Department of the State—Member

(iii) Secretary in-charge of the department dealing with consumer affairs in the State—Member.]

(2) The salary or honorarium and other allowances payable to, and the other terms and conditions of service [3][* * *] of the members of the State Commission shall be such as may be prescribed by the State Government.

[2][(3) Every member of the State Commission shall hold office for a term of five years or up to the age of sixty-seven years, whichever is earlier and shall not be eligible for re-appointment.

(4) Notwithstanding anything contained in sub-section (3), a person appointed as a President or as a member before the commencement of the Consumer Protection (Amendment) Act, 1993, shall continue to hold such office as President or member, as the case may be, till the completion of his term.

17. Jurisdiction of the State Commission

Subject to the other provisions of this Act, the State Commission shall have jurisdiction—

(a) to entertain—

(i) complaints where the value of the goods or services and compensation, if any, claimed exceeds rupees [1][five lakhs but does not exceed rupees twenty lakhs;] and

(ii) appeals against the orders of any District Forum within the State.

(b) to call for the records and pass appropriate orders in any consumer dispute which is pending before or has been decided by any District Forum within the State where it appears to the State Commission that such District Forum has exercised a jurisdiction not vested in it by law, or has failed to exercise a jurisdiction so vested or has acted in exercise on its jurisdiction illegally or with material irregularity.

18. Procedure Applicable to State Commission

[1][The provisions of Sections 12, 13 and 14 and the rules made thereunder] for the disposal of complaint by the Districts Forum shall, with such modification as may be necessary, be applicable to the disposal of disputes by the State Commission:

[5][**18A.** Vacancy in the office of the President. When the office of the President of the District Forum or of the State Commission, as the case may be, is vacant or when any such President is, by reason of absence or otherwise, unable to perform the duties of his office, the duties of the office shall be performed by such person, who is qualified to be appointed as President of the District Forum or, as the case may be, of the State Commission, as the State Government may appoint for the purpose.]

19. Appeals

Any person aggrieved by an order made by the State Commission in exercise of its powers conferred by sub-clause (i) of clause (a) of Section 17 may prefer an appeal against such order to the National Commission within a period of thirty days from the date of the order in such form and manner as may be prescribed:

Provided that the National Commission may entertain an appeal after the expiry of the said period of thirty days if it is satisfied that there was sufficient cause for not filing it within that period.

20. Composition of the National Commission

(1) The National Commission shall consist of—

(a) a person who is or has been a Judge of the Supreme Court, to be appointed by the Central Government, who shall be its President:

[2][Provided that no appointment under this clause shall be made except after consultation with the Chief Justice of India;]

(b) four other members who shall be persons of ability, integrity and standing and have adequate knowledge or experience of, or have shown capacity in dealing with, problems relating to economics, law, commerce, accountancy, industry, public affairs or administration, one of whom shall be a woman:

[2][Provided that every appointment under this clause shall be made by the Central Government on the recommendation of a selection committee consisting of the following, namely,—

(a) a person who is a Judge of the Supreme Court, to be nominated by the Chief Justice of India—Chairman,
(b) the Secretary in the Department of Legal Affairs in the Government of India—Member.]

(2) The salary or honorarium and other allowances payable to and the other terms and conditions of service [3][* * *] of the members of the National Commission shall be such as may be prescribed by the Central Government.

[2][(3) Every member of the National Commission shall hold office for a term of five years or up to the age of seventy years, whichever is earlier and shall not be eligible for re-appointment.

(4) Notwithstanding anything contained in sub-section (3), a person appointed as a President or as a member before the commencement of the Consumer Protection (Amendment) Act, 1993, shall continue to hold such office as President or member, as the case may be, till the completion of his term.]

21. Jurisdiction of the National Commission

Subject to the other provisions of this Act, the National Commission shall have jurisdiction—

(a) to entertain—

(i) complaints where the value of the goods or services and compensation, if any, claimed exceeds rupees [1][twenty lakhs]; and

(ii) appeals against the orders of any State Commission.

(b) to call for the records and pass appropriate orders in any consumer dispute which is pending before or has been decided by any State Commission where it appears to the National Commission that such State Commission has exercised a jurisdiction not vested in it by law, or has failed to exercise a jurisdiction so vested, or has acted in the exercise of its jurisdiction illegally or with material irregularity.

22. Power and Procedure Applicable to the National Commission

The National Commission shall, in the disposal of any complaints or of any proceedings before it, have

(a) the powers of a civil court as specified in sub-sections (4), (5) and (6) of Section 13;

(b) the power to issue an order to the opposite party directing him to do any one or more of the things referred to in clauses (a) to (i) of sub-section (1) of Section 14, and follow such procedure as may be prescribed by the Central Government.

23. Appeal

Any person, aggrieved by an order made by the National Commission in exercise of its powers conferred by sub-clause (i) of clause (a) of Section 21, may prefer an appeal against such order to the Supreme Court within a period of thirty days from the date of the order:

Provided that the Supreme Court may entertain an appeal after the expiry of the said period of thirty days if it is satisfied that there was sufficient cause for not filing it within that period.

24. Finality of Order

Every order of a District Forum, State Commission or the National

Commission shall, if no appeal has been preferred against such order under the provisions of this Act, be final.

[2][24A. Limitation Period

(1) The District Forum, the State Commission or the National Commission shall not admit a complaint unless it is filed within two years from the date on which the cause of action has arisen.

(2) Notwithstanding anything contained in sub-section (1), a complaint may be entertained after the period specified in sub-section (1), if the complainant satisfies the District Forum, the State Commission or the National Commission, as the case may be, that he had sufficient cause for not filing the complaint within such period:

Provided that no such complaint shall be entertained unless the National Commission, the State Commission or the District Forum, as the case may be, records its reasons for condoning such delay.

24B. Administrative Control

(1) The National Commission shall have administrative control over all the State Commissions in the following matters, namely—

(i) calling for periodical returns regarding the institution, disposal, pendency of cases;

(ii) issuance of instructions regarding adoption of uniform procedure in the hearing of matters, prior service of copies of documents produced by one party to the opposite parties, furnishing of English translation of judgments written in any language, speedy grant of copies of documents; and

(iii) generally overseeing the functioning of the State Commissions or the District Fora to ensure that the objects and purposes of the Act are best served without in any way interfering with their quasi-judicial freedom.

(2) The State Commission shall have administrative controls over all the District Fora within its jurisdiction in all matters referred to in sub-section (1).]

25. Enforcement of Orders by the Forum, the State Commission or the National Commission

Every order made by the District Forum, the State Commission or the National Commission, may be enforced by the District Forum, the State Commission or the National Commission as the case may be, in the same manner as if it were a decree or order made by a court in a suit pending therein and it shall be lawful for the District Forum, the State Commission or the National Commission to send, in the event of its inability to execute it, such order to the court within the local limits of whose jurisdiction—

(a) in the case of an order against a company, the registered office of the company is situated, or

(b) in the case of an order against any other person, the place where the person concerned voluntarily resides or carries on business or personally works for gain, is situated, and thereupon, the court to which the order is so sent, shall execute the order as if it were a decree or order sent to it for execution.

[1][26. Dismissal of Frivolous or Vexatious Complaints

Where a complaint instituted before the District Forum, the State Commission or, as the case may be, the National Commission, is found to be frivolous or vexatious, it shall, for reasons to be recorded in writing, dismiss the complaint and make an order that the complainant shall pay to the opposite party such cost, not exceeding ten thousand rupees, as may be specified in the order.

27. Penalties

Where a trader or a person against whom a complaint is made [2][or the complainant] fails or omits to comply with any order made by the District Forum, the State Commission or the National Commission, as the case may be, such trader or person [2][or complainant] shall be punishable with imprisonment for a term which shall not be less than one month but which may extend to three years, or with fine which shall not be less than two thousand rupees but which may extend to ten thousand rupees, or with both:

Provided that the District Forum, the State Commission or the National Commission, as the case may be, may, if it is satisfied that the circumstances of any case so require, impose a sentence of imprisonment or fine, or both, for a term lesser than minimum term and the amount lesser than the minimum amount, specified in this section.

CHAPTER IV: MISCELLANEOUS

28. Protection of Action taken in Good Faith

No suit, prosecution or other legal proceedings shall lie against the members of the District Forum, the State Commissions or the National Commission or any officer or person acting under the direction of the District Forum, the State Commission or the National Commission for executing any order made by it or in respect of anything which is in good faith done or intended to be done by such member, officer or person under this Act or under any rule or order made thereunder.

29. Power to Remove Difficulties

(1) If any difficulty arises in giving effect to the provisions of this Act, the Central Government may, by order in the Official Gazette, make such provisions not inconsistent with the provisions of this Act as appear to it to be necessary or expedient for removing the difficulty:

Provided that no such order shall be made after the expiry of a period of two years from the commencement of this Act.

(2) Every order made under this section shall, as soon as may be after it is made, be laid before each House of Parliament.

[5][**29A.** Vacancies or defects in appointment not to invalidate orders. No act or proceeding of the Districts Forum, the State Commission or the National Commission shall be invalid by reason only of the existence of any vacancy amongst its members or any defect in the constitution thereof.]

30. Power to Make Rules

(1) The Central Government may, by notification, make rules for carrying out the provisions contained in [2][clause (a) of sub-section (1) of Section 2], clause (b) of sub-section (2) of

Section 4, sub-section (2) of Section 5, clause (vi) of sub-section (4) of Section 13, Section 19, sub-section (2) of Section 20 and Section 22 of this Act.

(2) The State Government may, by notification, make rules for carrying out the provisions contained in [2][clause (b) of sub-section (2) and sub-section (4) of Section 7], sub-section (3) of Section 10, clause (c) of sub-section (1) of Section 13, sub-section (3) of Section 14, Section 15 and sub-section (2) of Section 16.

31. Laying of Rules

(1) Every rule made by the Central Government under this Act shall be laid, as soon as may be after it is made, before each House of Parliament, while it is in session, for a total period of thirty days which may be comprised in one session or in two or more successive sessions, and if, before the expiry of the session immediately following the session or the successive sessions aforesaid, both Houses agree in making any modification in the rule or both Houses agree that the rule should not be made, the rule shall thereafter have effect only in such modified form or be of no effect, as the case may be; so, however, that any such modification or annulment shall be without prejudice to the validity of anything previously done under that rule.

(2) Every rule made by a State Government under this Act shall be laid as soon as may be after it is made, before the State Legislature.

Appendix II

Government of India National Consumer Disputes Redressal Commission

[New Delhi, the 31st May, 2005]

NOTIFICATION

G.S.R. 342(E)—In exercise of the powers conferred by Section 30A of the Consumer Protection Act, 1986 (68 of 1986), the National Consumer Disputes Redressal Commission with the previous approval of the Central Government, hereby makes the following regulations, namely:

1. Short Title and Commencement—(1) These regulations may be called the Consumer Protection Regulations, 2005.

(2) They shall come into force on the date of their publication in the Official Gazette.

2. Definitions—In these regulations unless the context otherwise requires,—

(a) "*Act*" means the Consumer Protection Act, 1986 (68 of 1986);

(b) "*Consumer Forum*" means a District Forum. A Consumer Disputes Redressal Commission established in a State under clause (b) of Section 9 (hereafter called the State Commission) or the National Consumer Disputes Redressal Commission;

(c) "*Registrar*" means the head of the ministerial establishment of the Consumer Forum and exercising such powers and functions as are conferred upon him by the President of the Consumer Forum:

(d) "*rules*" means the rules made under the Act;

(e) "*section*" means a section of the Act;

(f) words and expressions used in these regulations and not defined herein but defined either in the Act or in the rules shall have the same meaning respectively assigned to them either in the Act or in the rules, as the case may be.

3. Arrangements in Consumer Forum—(1) A Consumer Forum, being not a regular court, shall have the arrangements as to depict it distinct from a court.

(2) In the hall in which the Consumer Forum shall hear the parties, the dais may not be kept more than 30 cm. in height than the place earmarked for the parties to occupy.

(3) At the dais of the hall, the President and the members of the Consumer Forum shall use the same type of chairs at the same level and these chairs need not have high backs.

4. Dress Code—(1) The President and members of every Consumer Forum while presiding over the Benches,—

(a) shall wear simple and sober dress;

(b) shall not wear—

(i) flashy dress or dress display any affluence;

(ii) Jeans or T-shirts.

(iii) as if they are holding Courts as Judges of a High Court or a District Court.

(2) The advocates shall be allowed to appear in the usual dress as prescribed by the High Court but without the gown.

5. Hearing Hours—Subject to the provisions of the rules, the normal working hours of the Consumer Forum for hearing matters shall be from 10.30 a.m to 1.00 p.m and 2.00 p.m to 4.00 p.m on all working days of the Central Government in the case of the National Commission and on all working days of the State Government in the case of the State Commission and the District Forum.

6. Cause List—(1) Cause list of the Consumer Forum for the following entire week shall be made ready before the close of the working hours of the preceding week and displayed on the notice board. The cause list in respect of a Consumer Forum having a website shall also be hosted on the website.

(2) Cause list shall be split into three different parts, namely:

(i) Admission and after notice matters;

(ii) Matters where evidence is to be recorded;

(iii) Final disposal matters.

(3) Every cause list shall contain the following particulars, namely:

(i) Sl. No. (ii) No. of the matter (iii) Names of the parties (iv) Name of the party or Counsel or agent appearing.

(4) If a date of hearing is given in the presence of parties or their agents, it shall not be a ground for non-appearance for the reason that the cause list for the concerned date does not show the matter or contains incorrect entry or there is omission of the particulars of the matter.

7. Institution of complaints, appeals and revision petitions— (1) Where a complaint is filed in District Forum or State Commission it shall be filed in three sets and where it is filed in the National Commission it shall be filed in four sets with additional sets equal to the number of opposite party(ies)/respondent(s).

(2) Every complaint shall clearly contain particulars of dispute and the relief claimed and shall also be accompanied by copies of such documents as are necessary to prove the claim made in the complaint.

8. Nomenclature to be given to the complaints, appeals and revisions petition—(1) A complaint shall hereinafter be referred to as Consumer Complaint (C.C.) instead of O.P., e.g., C.C. No.2 of 2005.

(2) An appeal shall be referred to as F.A., Revision Petition as R.P., Execution. Application as E.A, Transfer Application T.A. and Review as RA containing the number and the year of filing.

9. Scrutiny of complaint, appeal, petition and revision petition—(1) Every complaint, appeal, or revision petition shall after it is filed be numbered by the Registrar.

(2) If there is any defect in the filing of the complaint, appeal or revision petition, the particulars of such defects shall be recorded and the party or his agents shall be informed of the defects asking them for removing the defects within 15 days.

(3) In case the party disputes in the correctness of the defects pointed out the matter shall be placed before the Consumer Forum for appropriate orders.

(4) After the expiry of the time given, the matter shall, irrespective of the fact as to whether the defects have been removed or not, be placed before the Consumer Forum for appropriate orders.

(5) If the objections raised by the Registrar are substantial and are not removed within the time allowed for the purpose, those days shall not be excluded for counting the period of limitation.

(6) As required by the second proviso to sub-section (3) of Section 12, the admissibility of the complaint shall ordinarily be

decided within twenty-one days from the date on which the complaint was received.

(7) In case any defect is pointed out by the Registrar, twenty-one days from the date on which such defect was removed shall be reckoned for the purpose of sub-regulation (5).

(8) All pending complaints, appeals and revision petitions which have not come up for admission till the date of commencement of these regulations and are pending for admission for more than 21 days shall be listed immediately by the Consumer Forum for admission and not later than 21 days from the date of commencement of these regulations.

10. Issue of Notice—(1) Whenever, the Consumer Forum directs the issuance of a notice in respect of a complaint, appeal or revision petition, as the case may be, to the opposite party(ies)/respondent(s), ordinarily such notice shall be issued for a period of 30 days and depending upon the circumstances of each case even for less than 30 days.

(2) When there is a question of raising presumption of service, 30 days notice shall be required.

(3) Whenever, notices are sought to be effected by a courier service, it shall be ascertained that the courier is of repute.

(4) While appointing the courier for the purpose of effecting service, security deposit may also be taken.

(5) Along with the notice, copies of the complaint, memorandum of grounds of appeal, petitions as the case may be and other documents filed shall be served upon the opposite party(ies)/respondent(s).

(6) After the opposite party or respondent has put in appearance, no application or document shall be received by the Registrar unless it bears an endorsement that a copy thereof has been served upon the other side.

11. Adjournment—(1) Every proceeding before a Consumer Forum shall be conducted as expeditiously as possible and as per the requirements of the Act.

(2) The Consumer Forum shall record the reasons for any adjournment made by it.

(3) The cost of adjournment, if asked by the opposite party or parties, shall not be less than five hundred rupees per adjournment and could be more depending upon the value and nature of the complaint as may be decided by the Consumer Forum.

(4) The complainant, appellant or petitioner, as the case may be, may also be burdened with cost unless sufficient cause is shown for seeking adjournment:

Provided that in the circumstances of a particular case, the amount of cost imposed may be less than five hundred rupees but in no case less than one hundred rupees.

(5) The cost imposed may be given to the other party or parties to defray his or their expenses or be deposited in the Consumer Legal Aid Account to be maintained by the respective Consumer Forum, as the Consumer Forum may order.

(6) If any adjournment is granted without awarding cost, the order sheet shall mention the reasons thereof.

(7) All orders adjourning the matter shall be signed by the President and members constituting the Bench and not by the Court Master or Bench Clerk.

(8) Non-availability of a lawyer who is representing the party shall not be a ground for seeking adjournment of the matter unless absence is beyond the control of the lawyer such as his sudden illness or bereavement in the family.

12. Hearing by Benches—Where a Bench, constituted by the President of the State Commission or the National Commission as provided under Section 16 or Section 20, as the case may be, does not have a member with judicial background and any complex question of law arises and there is no precedent to decide the law point, the Bench so constituted may refer the matter to the President of the State Commission or the National Commission as the case may be to constitute another Bench of which the President shall be a member.

13. Arguments—(1) Arguments should be as brief as possible and to the point at issue.

(2) Where a party is represented by a counsel, it shall be mandatory to file a brief of written arguments two days before the matter is fixed for arguments.

(3) In case of default to file briefs, the cost shall be imposed at the same rates as laid down for grant of adjournments.

14. Limitations—(1) Subject to the provisions of Sections 15, 19 and 24A, the period of limitation in the following matters shall be as follows:

(i) Revision Petition shall be filed within 90 days from the date of the order or the date of receipt of the order as the case may be;

(ii) Application for setting aside the *ex parte* order under Section 22A or dismissal of the complaint in default shall be maintainable if filed within thirty days from the date of the order or date of receipt of the order, as the case may be;

(iii) An application for review under sub-section (2) of Section 22 shall be filed to the National Commission within 30 days from the date of the order or receipt of the order, as the case may be;

(iv) The period of limitation for filing any application for which no period of limitation has been specified in the Act, the rules of these regulations shall be thirty days from the date of the cause of action or the date of knowledge.

(2) Subject to the provisions of the Act, the Consumer Forum may condone the delay in filing an application or a petition referred to in sub-regulation (1) if valid and sufficient reasons to its satisfaction are given.

15. Review—(1) It shall set out clearly the grounds for review.

(2) Unless otherwise ordered by the National Commission, an application for review shall be disposed off by circulation without oral arguments, as far as practicable between the same members who had delivered the order sought to be reviewed.

16. Appearance of Voluntary Consumer Organisations—(1) Recognised Consumer Organisations have a right of audience before the Consumer Forum.

(2) An authorisation of a Voluntary Consumer Organisation may be by way of special power of attorney executed on a non-judicial paper or even on plain paper duly attested by a Gazetted Officer or a Notary Public.

(3) The Power of Attorney holder shall be entitled to engage a counsel, if authorised to do so.

(4) A Voluntary Consumer Organisation can engage a counsel or an advocate of its choice or it can itself represent through one of its office bearers as per the rules governing it.

(5) In case of a complaint where the Voluntary Consumer Organisation is a complainant along with the consumer himself and the dispute affects the complainant individually, he can withdraw the complaint:

Provided that if the issue involves unfair trade practice or restrictive trade practice a Voluntary Consumer Organisation may continue to proceed with the complaint even if the complainant wishes to withdraw the same.

(6) A Consumer Forum has to guard itself from touts and busy bodies in the garb of power of attorney holders or authorised agents in the proceedings before it.

(7) While a Consumer Forum may permit an authorised agent to appear before it, but authorised agent shall not be one who has used this as a profession:

Provided that this sub-regulation shall not apply in case of advocates.

(8) An authorised agent may be debarred from appearing before a Consumer Forum if he is found guilty of misconduct or any other malpractice at any time.

17. *Ex-parte* Interim Order—Any *ex-parte* interim order issued by the Consumer Forum shall stand vacated after 45 days if in the meanwhile the objections to the interim order are not heard and disposed of.

18. Final Order—(1) An order on the top right hand corner shall show as to when the complaint was filed and the date of the order.

(2) The cause title of the order shall contain the names of all the parties with their addresses.

(3) In the body of the order it is desirable that after mentioning the complainant or the opposite party, their names as shown in the title be mentioned and parties thereafter may not be mentioned as complainant or opposite party No.1 or opposite party No.2, etc.

(4) The cause title shall also clearly show if the appellant or respondent was the complainant or opposite party.

(5) The order of a Consumer Forum disposing of a matter shall be as short and precise as practicable and unnecessary long quotations from the judgments of the higher courts or otherwise shall be avoided.

(6) When a copy of the order is sent to a party, the mode by which it is sent and the date on which it is sent shall be stamped on the last page of the order.

(7) The Consumer Forum shall pass final order invariably within fifteen days of the conclusion of the arguments.

19. Return on Institution and Disposal of Cases—(1) A Consumer Forum is expected to dispose of at least 75 to 100 matters every month.

(2) A periodic monthly return of institution and disposal of cases shall be sent by the District Forums to the State Commission.

(3) The State Commission shall submit a periodic monthly return of institution and disposal of cases to the National Commission.

(4) Notwithstanding anything contained in this regulation, the President of the National Commission may, at any time, call for any return or information relating to its functioning from a State Commission or District Forums.

20. Preservation of Records—(1) In the case of complaint, the record containing main files with original order sheet shall be preserved for a period of five years.

(2) In the case of records of first appeal and revision petitions, it shall be preserved for three years from the date of disposal of the appeal or revision as the case may be.

(3) Immediately after the consumer complaint, first appeal or revision petition, as the case may be, is disposed of, extra sets shall be given to the parties who may use the same for filing of appeal or revision petition and in that case the necessity to summon the record from the forums below can be dispensed with.

(4) The Registrar shall inform the parties while forwarding the certified copy of the final order, where they do not appear in person at the time of finally disposing of the matter to arrange to collect the extra sets.

(5) A period of at least one month shall be given for the purpose of collection of records by the party and in case of default the extra sets shall be weeded out.

21. Certified Copy—(l) A copy of the order is to be given to the parties free of cost as required under the Act and the rules made thereunder.

(2) In case a party requires an extra copy, it shall be issued to him duly certified by the Registry on a payment of Rs. 20 irrespective of number of pages.

(3) A certified copy of an order shall clearly specify the date when free copy was issued, date of application, date when the copy was made ready and the date when it was so delivered to him.

(4) A fee of Rs. 20 shall be paid for obtaining another certified copy.

(5) Any party desiring to get a certified copy of any document on the file of the Consumer Forum, may get the same on payment

of certification fee of twenty rupees per copy. Provided that if any such document of which certified copy is sought, is over and above 5 pages, an extra amount of one rupee per page shall be charged over and above the fee of twenty rupees.

(6) Certified copy of any miscellaneous order passed by the Consumer Forum shall be supplied on payment of Rs. 5 per copy.

22. Inspection of Records—Parties or their agents can inspect the records of any matter by filing an application on payment often rupees as fee.

23. Filing of Criminal Complaint—Wherever a complaint is required to be filed by the Consumer Forum under sub-section (5) of Section 13, the Consumer Forum may authorise its Registrar to file the complaint.

24. Practice Directions—The National Commission shall be entitled to issue practice directions from time-to-time as may be necessary for the proper conduct of the cases before Consumer Forum including prescribing forms for complaints, notices, returns, certificate to be issued to the collector and the like.

25. Parcsha Yad-dast—Where a party appears in person and is illiterate, the Court Master or Bench Clerk shall give to that party the next date of hearing in writing.

26. Miscellaneous—(1) In all proceedings before the Consumer Forum, endeavour shall be made by the parties and their counsel to avoid the use of provisions of Code of Civil Procedure, 1908 (5 of 1908):

Provided that the provisions of the Code of Civil Procedure, 1908 may be applied which have been referred to in the Act or in the rules made thereunder.

(2) Every State Commission and every District Forum shall take steps for its computerisation and networking.

(3) The Consumer Forum shall give proper respect and courtesy to the parties who appear in person and shall provide separate accommodation in the Hall for the convenience of the parties.

(4) The Consumer Forum shall not insist upon the parties to engage advocates.

(5) The Fees collected for inspection of the documents and supply of certified copies shall be deposited in the account maintained for the purpose of depositing fee for filing a complaint as prescribed by the Central Government by rules.

(6) The cases filed by or against the senior citizens, physically challenged, widows and persons suffering from serious ailments shall be listed and disposed of on a priority basis.

[F.No.A-105/NCDRC/2005]
(B.V. SHARMA)
Joint Registrar

Appendix III

Address of Consumer Courts in India

Address of National Consumer Disputes Redressal Commission in India

National Consumer Disputes Redressal Commission,
A Wing, 5th Floor, Janpath Bhawan,
Cannaught Place, New Delhi-110001.
Fax: (011) 23712456

Addresses of State Consumer Disputes Redressal Commissions in India

Andhra Pradesh

The President,
State Consumer Disputes Redressal Commission,
High Court Building, Hyderabad-500 002.

Arunachal Pradesh

The President,
Arunachal Pradesh State Consumer Disputes Redressal Commission,
65 Vivek Vihar,
Itanagar-795 111.

Assam

The President,
Assam State Consumer Disputes Redressal Commission,
Guwahati High Court,
Guwahati.

Bihar

The President,
Bihar State Consumer Disputes Redressal Commission,
12, North Shrikrishnapuri, Patna.

Delhi

Delhi State Consumer Disputes Redressal Commission,
A-Block, Vikas Bhawan,
I.P. Estate, New Delhi.
Tel: 23322946, 23322989, 23321558.

Goa

The President,
Goa State Consumer Disputes Redressal Commission,
C/o Directorate of Civil Supplies and Price Control,
Janta House, Panaji, Goa.

Gujarat

The President,
Gujarat State Consumer Disputes Redressal Commission,
4, Vijay Park Society, Opp. Municipal Market,
Navrangpura, Ahemdabad-380009.

Haryana

The President,
Haryana State Consumer Disputes Redressal Commission,
Kothi No. 548, Sector 8B, Chandigarh-160 018.

Himachal Pradesh

The President,
H.P. State Consumer Disputes Commission,
Mini Secretariat,
Shimla-171 002.

Karnataka

The President,
Karnataka State Consumer Disputes Redressal Commission,
Basava, Basaveswara Circle,
Miller Road, Banglore-560 001.

Kerala

The President,
State Consumer Disputes Rerdressal Commission,
T.C.14/407, Extra Police Road,
Palayam, Museum P.O.
Thiruvananthapuram-695 033.

Madhya Pradesh

The President,
Madhya Pradesh State Consumer Disputes Redressal Commission,
Plot No. N-24, Zone-I Maharana Pratap Nagar,
Bhopal-462 011.

Maharashtra

The President,
Maharashtra State Consumer Disputes Redressal Commission,
Administrative College, Room Nos.1 and 2,
Hazarimal Somani Marg,
Opp. V.T. Station, Bombay-400 001.

Manipur

The President,
Manipur State Consumer Disputes Redressal Forum,
Post Box No. 64, Imphal.

Meghalaya

The President,
Meghalaya State Consumer Disputes Redressal Commission,

C/o Office of the Transport Commissioner,
Lower Luchumiere, Shillong-793 001.

Mizoram

The President,
Mizoram State Consumer Disputes Redressal Commission,
Zodian Square, Aizawal-796 001, Mizoram.

Nagaland

The President,
Nagaland State Consumer Disputes Redressal Commission,
Guwahati High Court Building, Guwahati

Orissa

President,
Orissa State Consumer Disputes Redressal Commission,
High Court Building, Cuttack-753 001.

Punjab

The President,
Punjab State Consumer Disputes Redressal Commission,
SCO No. 3009010, Sector 22-D, Chandigarh.

Rajasthan

The President,
Rajasthan State Consumer Disputes Redressal Commission,
Room No. 133, 1st Floor, SSO Building, Secretariat
Jaipur (Rajasthan)

Sikkim

The President,
Sikkim State Consumer Disputes Redressal Commission,
C/o Office of Food & Civil Supplies Department, Gangtok.

Tamil Nadu

The President,
Tamil Nadu State Consumer Disputes Redressal Commission,
212, R.K. Mutt Road, Slum Clearence Board Building,
IInd Floor, Southern Wing, Mylapore, Madras-600 004.

Tripura

The President,
Tripura State Consumer Disputes Redressal Commission,
307, Akhura Road, Agartala-799 001 (Tripura)

Uttar Pradesh

The President,
Uttar Pradesh State Consumer Disputes Redressal Commission,
2A/1, Rana Pratap Marg, Lucknow (UP)

West Bengal

The President,
West Bengal State Consumer Disputes Redressal Commission,
Bhabani Bhavan, Ground Floor, Calcutta-700 027.

Andaman & Nicobar Islands

President,
Andaman & Nicobar State Consumer Disputes Redressal Commission,
Andaman & Nicobar Islands, Port Blair.

Chandigarh Administration

The President,
Chandigarh State Consumer Disputes Redressal Commission,
District Court Complex, New, IIIrd Floor,
Sector-17, Chandigarh-160 017.

Dadar & Nagar Haveli

The President,
Dadra & Nagar Haveli State Consumer Disputes Redressal Commission,
Municipal Council Hall, Daman.

Daman and Diu

The President,
Daman & Diu State Consumer Disputes Redressal Commission,
Bunglows No. 45/1, Civil Lines, Nagpur-440 001.

Delhi

The President,
Delhi State Consumer Disputes Redressal Commission,
Vikas Bhawan, Near C.R. Building,
I.P. Estate, New Delhi-110 002.

Lakshadweep

The President,
Lakshadweep State Consumer Disputes Redressal Commission,
U.T. of Lakshadweep, Kavaratti-682 555

Pondicherry

The President,
Pondicherry State Consumer Disputes Redressal Commission,
No. 46, Gubert Avenue (Beach Road), Pondicherry.

Index